# Empower ADHD Kids!

## Practical Strategies to Assist Children with Attention Deficit Hyperactivity Disorder in Developing Learning and Social Competencies

by
Becky Daniel-White

illustrated by
Kathryn E. Flora

**Publisher**
Key Education Publishing Company, LLC
Minneapolis, Minnesota

◇◇◇◇◇◇◇◇◇◇◇◇◇◇◇◇◇◇◇◇◇◇◇◇◇◇◇◇◇◇◇◇◇◇◇◇◇◇◇◇◇◇◇◇◇◇◇◇◇◇◇◇◇◇◇◇◇

# FOOTNOTE REFERENCES *

Page 5......*Ritalin Free Kids*, by Judyth Reichenberg-Ullman, N.D., M.S.W. and Robert Ullman, N.D. (Prima Publishing, © 2000), Introduction

Page 6.....AdhdNews.com, What Is ADHD? (Alternative ADHD Treatments)

Page 7.....Ibid

Page 8.....Ibid

Page 9.....*The Misunderstood Child: Understanding and Coping with Your Child's Learning Disabilities*, (Third Edition) by Larry B. Silver, M.D., (Random House Publishers, © 1998), p. 3

Page 11...*ADHD: A Complete and Authoritative Guide*, by Michael I. Reiff, MD, with Sherill Tippins, (American Academy of Pediatrics, © 2004) p. 320

Page 12...*Ritalin Free Kids*, p. 44

Page 13...*Ritalin Free Kids*, p. 25

Page 15...*Taking Charge of ADHD*, by Russell A. Barkley, PhD, (The Guilford Press, © 2000), p. 119

Page 16...*Taking Charge of ADHD*, p. 77

Page 18...*Ritalin Free Kids*, p. 13

Page 21...*ADHD: A Complete and Authoritative Guide*, p. 165

Page 23...*Ritalin Free Kids*, p. 3

Page 24...*All About Attention Deficit Disorder*, p. 24

Page 25...*The Misunderstood Child*, p. 112.

Page 26...*The Parent's Guide to Attention Deficit Disorders*, (Second Edition) by Stephen B. McCarney, Ed.D and Angela Marie Bauer, M.Ed., (Hawthorne Educational Services Inc., © 1995), p. 148

Page 27...*ADHD: A Complete and Authoritative Guide*, p. 229

Page 29...*The Parent's Guide to Attention Deficit Disorders*, p. 33

Page 30...*All About Attention Deficit Disorder,*(Second Edition), Thomas W. Phelan, Ph.D. (Child Management Inc., © 2000), p. 28

Page 32...*The Misunderstood Child*, p. 257

Page 33...*Ritalin Free Kids*, p. 95

Page 34...*All About Attention Deficit Disorder*, p. 27

Page 29...*The Parent's Guide to Attention Deficit Disorders*, p. 60

Page 36...*Taking Charge of ADHD*, p. 36

Page 39...*The Parent's Guide to Attention Deficit Disorders*, p. 233

Page 39...*The A.D.D. Book*, by William Sears, M.D., and Lynda Thompson, Ph.D. (Little, Brown, and Company, © 1998), p. 28

Page 40...*The Parent's Guide to Attention Deficit Disorders*, p. 233

Page 41...*All About Attention Deficit Disorder*, p. 23

Page 42...*The Misunderstood Child*, p. 217

Page 43...*The A.D.D. Book*, p. 108

Page 45...*The Parent's Guide to Attention Deficit Disorders*, p. 119

Page 46...*The Parent's Guide to Attention Deficit Disorders*, p. 249

Page 47...*The Parent's Guide to Attention Deficit Disorders*, p. 141

Page 48...*The A.D.D. Book*, p. 104

Page 50...*ADHD: A Complete and Authoritative Guide*, p. 104

Page 51...*The Misunderstood Child*, p. 376

Page 52...*The Misunderstood Child*, p. 96

Page 55...Pay Attention!!! p. 32

Page 56...*All About Attention Deficit Disorder*, p. 65

Page 57...*The Misunderstood Child*, p. 376

Page 59...*All About Attention Deficit Disorder*, p. 199

Page 60...AdhdNews.com, What Is ADHD? (Alternative ADHD Treatments)

Page 61...*ADHD: A Complete and Authoritative Guide*, p. 97

## CONGRATULATIONS ON YOUR PURCHASE OF A KEY EDUCATION PRODUCT!

The editors at Key Education are former teachers who bring experience, enthusiasm, and quality to each and every product. Thousands of teachers have looked to the staff at Key Education for new and innovative resources to make their work more enjoyable and rewarding. Key Education is committed to developing and publishing educational materials that will assist teachers in building a strong and developmentally appropriate curriculum for young children.

### PLAN FOR GREAT TEACHING EXPERIENCES WHEN YOU USE
### EDUCATIONAL MATERIALS FROM KEY EDUCATION PUBLISHING COMPANY, LLC.

Standard Book Number:1-933052-06-6
*Empower ADHD Kids!*
Copyright © 2005
by Key Education Publishing Company, LLC
Minneapolis, Minnesota 55431

**Printed in the USA • All rights reserved**

**Credits**
Author: Becky Daniel-White
Project Director: Sherrill B. Flora
Illustrator: Kathryn E. Flora
Cover Design: Mary Claire
Editors: George C. Flora
         Bernadette Baczynski
Photography: © Comstock
             © Brand X Pictures
             © Rubberball
Production: Key Education Staff

Key Education welcomes manuscripts and product ideas from teachers. For a copy of our submission guidelines, please send a self-addressed, stamped envelope to:
**Key Education Publishing Company, LLC**
**Acquisitions Department • 9601 Newton Avenue South**
**Minneapolis, Minnesota 55431**

◇◇◇◇◇◇◇◇◇◇◇◇◇◇◇◇◇◇◇◇◇◇◇◇◇◇◇◇◇◇◇◇◇◇◇◇◇◇◇◇◇◇◇◇◇◇◇◇◇◇◇◇◇◇◇◇◇

# Introduction for Parents and Teachers

It's a fact: Attention Deficit Hyperactivity Disorder (ADHD) is the most common of the five major behavioral disorders that affect children ages five to eighteen. It is also very interesting to note that something else major happens to all children between the ages of five and eighteen. What is it? Simple–they go to school. Suddenly, children who have been allowed to move freely and make choices about their play are required to conform to a classroom setting. They are asked to sit quietly, listen, learn, and memorize facts that are not always of interest to them. Some children make the transition with ease, others do not. It's not surprising that attention deficit hyperactivity disorder is first diagnosed in early primary grades.

When dealing with children, the old adage "talk is cheap" isn't exactly timely or correct. When a child has a problem, talking about the problem and listening to the child's feelings is the first step to help the child cope and become empowered. Attention deficit hyperactivity disorder (ADHD) is no exception. The less of a mystery it is, the better.

On the negative side of the disorder are characteristics such as:
• attention deficit, which makes it difficult to focus, and
• hyperactivity, which makes sitting still long enough to learn extremely difficult.

It is important to let the child know that ADHD is a disorder, not a disability. ADHD may be inconvenient, but it isn't an excuse for not learning. It is vital that children with ADHD understand all aspects of the disorder so they can acquire the skills and the support system to help them learn and master social skills.

Children with ADHD often have low self-esteem. It is especially sad that children with ADHD have the added burden of thinking they are in some way not as good, smart, or as acceptable as other children. Further, teens with ADHD sometimes demonstrate addictive behaviors and have trouble with the law. It is crucial that teachers and parents help young children with ADHD focus on the positive aspects of the disorder so they can establish strong, healthy relationships.

**Begin by teaching children that many ADHD traits are positive.** Children with ADHD often have above average I.Q's and are usually highly creative, artistic, intuitive, inventive, and humorous. Many display other positive characteristics that make them special individuals. Helping each child celebrate the positive traits of ADHD will give them the pride and courage needed to face each day and grow up to be happy, productive adults.

*Author's Special Note:* Not all children with Attention Deficit Disorder (ADD) are hyperactive. To avoid redundancy in this book, Attention Deficit Disorder and Attention Deficit Hyperactivity Disorder (ADHD) will both be indicated by the acronym ADHD.

# Table of Contents

# CHAPTER ONE                ADHD—That's Me!

## What the Experts Say

Attention deficit hyperactivity disorder (ADHD) is the most common behavioral disorder in children. *

## Introducing the Concept

Many children with ADHD find school difficult, which often leads to poor self-concepts. From the very beginning, let the child know that although ADHD might make life difficult at times, there are tools that can change all of that and that you are willing to champion her in her quest for empowerment.

## Let's Talk About It

1. Do you know what ADHD is?
2. If you are ADHD, when did you first find out?
3. Did a teacher, doctor, or parent tell you?
4. Do you know that lots of children and adults are ADHD?

## Empowering Activity

Explain that ADHD is a small part of who the child is and that she has many other characteristics that make her unique. Convey the important message that being ADHD is okay by having her create an "All About Me!" collage.

*You will need:* A sheet of poster board (11 x 17 inches), old magazines, newspapers, scissors, glue stick, markers, glitter and photographs.

*Directions:* Have the child cut out words and pictures from magazines and newspapers that describe her, then arrange them in a pleasing way. Help her attach the appropriate words and pictures to the poster board. Use markers and glitter to add pizzazz to the collage. As the child learns ways to deal with her ADHD, she can place additional messages on the poster.

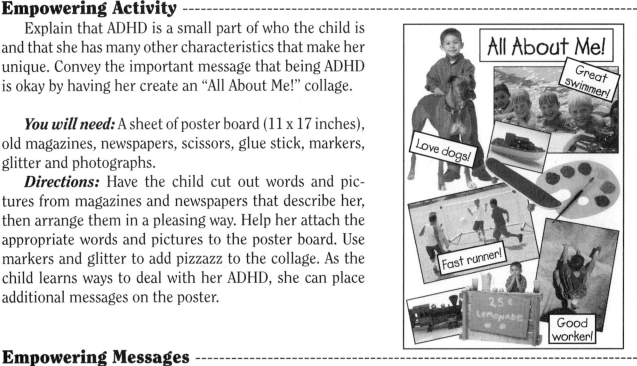

## Empowering Messages

*Adult:* The most important thing that you will ever teach a child with ADHD is that every part of her is acceptable to you—including her ADHD traits.

*Child:* Having ADHD is only one small part of who I am.

# A is for Attention

## What the Experts Say

The A in ADHD stands for Attention. "It's generally accepted that children with ADHD, attention deficit disorder, lack the ability to focus attention . . . ." *

## Introducing the Concept

It is never too early for children with ADHD to begin learning all they can about the disorder. The facts will help them understand themselves better so they can become responsible for their own behavior, learning, and socialization.

## Let's Talk About It

1. Do you know what the A in ADHD stands for?
2. What does attention mean?
3. How do you like your mother and father to pay attention to you?
4. Do you have a pet that you pay attention to? What do you do for the pet?

## Empowering Activity

Explain that in the days ahead, the child will be learning more about ADHD. Say, "It is good to learn all you can about ADHD." Ask, "What does the first A in ADHD stand for?" Review the definition of attention by playing a staring game called "Don't Blink." You only need two people to play the game.

***Directions:*** Players sit facing each other with their heads about two feet apart. At a given signal, players look into each other's eyes. The object of the game is not to blink or break the stare. The person who can hold her gaze and pay attention to the opponent the longest is declared the winner. Encourage her to play the game with other students, siblings, and parents. Practicing focusing in this way will help her develop skills needed to pay attention in other situations.

## Empowering Messages

***Adult:*** Focusing skills and broadening attention span are skills that you can help the child learn.
***Child:*** Even though it may be difficult for me to pay attention, I am still an extraordinary kid.

# D is for Deficit

## What the Experts Say

The D in ADHD stands for deficit. Children with ADHD are sometimes said to have a deficit in attention. It may be more accurately called "attention difficulty," because ADHD kids have difficulty paying attention to just one thing at a time. "ADHD symptoms . . . include: poor concentration and a brief attention span." *

## Introducing the Concept

Concentration is required for success in all areas of life. But a child can't pay attention just because she is told to do so. Children with ADHD need tools to help them cope with their attention deficit disorder.

## Let's Talk About It

1. Do you know what the first D in ADHD stands for?
2. What does deficit mean?
3. Have you ever been in a car with your dad when the car ran out of gas, or had a gas deficit?
4. Has your mother ever run out of bread while making your lunch, or had a bread deficit?
5. What do you think it means to have an attention deficit?

## Empowering Activity

Explain that everyone has trouble paying attention to things that don't interest them. Ask, "What are some things that you find difficult to pay attention to?" Discuss some things the child enjoys doing and can concentrate on for extended periods of time, such as playing video games or using a computer. Convey that the child already knows how to stay focused on many things she likes.

| Things That Hold My Attention | Things That Don't Hold My Attention |
|---|---|
| Computer | Reading |
| Video games | Sitting at desk |
| Art work | Homework |
| Playing outside | Waiting in line |
| Riding my bike | Boring movies |

***You will need:*** An 11 x 17 inch sheet of paper folded vertically, pencil, crayons or markers.

***Directions:*** On the upper left-hand side of the paper, write or help the child write: "Things That Hold My Attention." On the upper right-hand side of the paper, write: "Things That Don't Hold My Attention." Encourage the child to illustrate or list many examples of each.

## Empowering Messages

***Adult:*** Telling a child with ADHD to pay attention will not help her overcome her built-in attentional difference. Giving a child with ADHD opportunities to do high-interest activities will help increase her attention span.

***Child:*** I can pay attention to things that interest me. I can learn how to focus on other things as well.

# H is for Hyperactivity

## What the Experts Say

The H in ADHD stands for hyperactivity. For many children, hyperactivity becomes less prominent as they age. "For some there is remission at puberty, but for others the condition, if untreated, continues into adulthood." *

## Introducing the Concept

Hyperactive children rarely run in circles or up and down hallways. More often they fidget, squirm, and move in purposeless motions. Unable to stand or sit still very long, they can become disruptive to those around them. Usually the hyperactive child is unaware that she is exhibiting a disturbing behavior. It is helpful to name the disturbing behavior and give her a more acceptable energy outlet. Example: "Erica, you are drumming your pencil and the noise is disturbing those around you. I need you to stop. If you cannot hold your pencil still, please go outside and drum with your pencil."

## Let's Talk About It

1. Do you know what the H in ADHD stands for?
2. What does it mean to be hyperactive?
3. Do you have lots of energy to get up and go?
4. Do you like recess better than classroom study?

## Empowering Activity

Explain that there are many occupations, sports, and hobbies that require the participants to think fast and move quickly. For example, drummers have to move their hands at accelerated speeds. Say, "It isn't a bad thing to be able to move faster than most, but it can be disruptive to others when working in a group or family situation."

Playing a singing game to convey that excessive speed, when working in a group, can be disruptive.

***Directions:*** Pick one child to be "it." While the others sing a familiar song like "Twinkle, Twinkle, Little Star," "It" sings the song at an accelerate speed. Note how the person singing too fast disturbs the cadence of the other singers. Try with a variety of songs, and let everyone in the group have a chance to be It. Follow with a discussion about what happens when one person isn't keeping pace.

## Empowering Messages

***Adult:*** Telling a child with ADHD to sit still or stop fidgeting doesn't help her gain control. She needs to know the exact behavior that you are referring to and be given specific directions for changing the behavior.

***Child:*** I may move faster than others, but when working in a group, I know that I should keep pace.

# D Stands for Disorder

## What the Experts Say

The last D in ADHD stands for disorder, not disease, and ADHD is a disorder not a disease. "A neurological disorder . . . is the result of a nervous system that has been wired a little differently. . . . it processes information in a different way." *

## Introducing the Concept

Children with ADHD actually perceive things differently than others do. The message for this lesson is that there is not always a right or a wrong way to see things. There are only different ways of perceiving them.

## Let's Talk About It

1. What does the last D in ADHD stand for?
2. What is a disorder? Is a disorder the same thing as a disease?
3. Is there always a right and wrong way to see things?
4  Are there many different ways of seeing the same thing?
5. How does an ant see a grain of sugar? How do you see that same grain of sugar? Does the sugar change?

## Empowering Activity

To demonstrate that things may not always be as they appear, help the child make a pinwheel.

***You will need:*** The pinwheel example on this page, paper, scissors, blue and red crayons, sharpened pencil, brad fastener, and a plastic drinking straw.

### Directions:

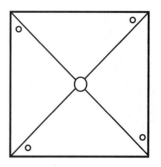

1. Enlarge and reproduce the pinwheel pattern and cut out on the solid lines.
2  Color one side of the pinwheel red and the other side blue.
3. Cut the diagonal lines from the corners to the center circle. Don't cut into the circle.
4. Help the child use the sharpened pencil to poke a hole through the four tiny dark circles.
5. The pencil point also works well to poke a hole in the straw about 1/2-inch from the top.
6. Make the tiny holes on the four points overlap consecutively and meet at the center circle.
7. Push the ends of the paper fastener through the holes in the pinwheel. Then push the fastener through the center circle.
8. Place the straw on the back side of the pinwheel and push the ends of the fastener through the hole in the straw. Open up the fastener and flatten the ends.
9. Blow on the pinwheel. Is it blue? Red? Purple? Watch the colors change.

## Empowering Messages

***Adult:*** Diverse perceptions make life interesting. Your child with ADHD may be a challenge, but life won't be boring.

***Child:*** ADHD isn't an illness; it's a personality type.

# KEYS TO SUCCESS #1

## Glancing Back

The lessons and activities you have just completed were designed to help the child define ADHD and establish a foundation for further understanding. As reminders of what has been learned, have her complete the Keys to Understanding and Empowering Self-Talk.

## Keys to Understanding ADHD

Reproduce the paper keys on card stock and laminate. At the top of each key, punch a hole where indicated. Place the keys on a large metal ring. The child will be adding other "Keys to Success" as future lessons are completed.

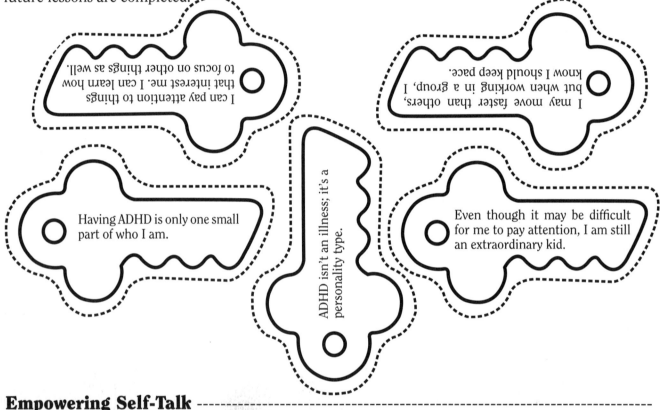

## Empowering Self-Talk

Have the student copy and cut out the words below. Tell her to put the words in her sock drawer. Every day as she puts on her shoes and socks to begin the day's journey, she is to repeat the words five times.

**My uniqueness makes me awesome!**

# Be Prepared

## What the Experts Say

It is helpful for children with ADHD to learn all they can about the condition. "Adults with ADHD are much more likely to enjoy successful and satisfying lives if they were properly prepared during childhood . . . to monitor and manage their symptoms on their own." *

## Introducing the Concept

Since ADHD is so widespread, you as the parent or teacher must be able to provide the knowledge and tools that the youngsters need in order to succeed. The more children with ADHD learn about the condition, the better they will be able to deal with the traits. List important key facts about ADHD on a chalkboard or a large sheet of paper and leave it up for awhile.

*Examples:*
- There are millions of children and adults with ADHD.
- Children can overcome ADHD traits.
- ADHD has beneficial characteristics.

## Let's Talk About It

1. What do you find annoying about being ADHD?
2. Is there anything you like about being ADHD?
3. How much do you know about ADHD?
4. How many ADHD characteristics can you name?
5. Have you ever discussed your ADHD with a parent or a friend?

## Empowering Activity

Depending upon how you view them, characteristics of ADHD can be negative or positive. Convey the positive aspects of ADHD by playing a word game.

*Directions:* On the chalkboard or a large sheet of paper, list ADHD traits and have the child provide additional positive words that can mean the same thing. Discuss times when each ADHD trait could be useful. Example: Talkative people sometimes become talk-show hosts, newscasters, or disc jockeys.

| ADHD Trait | More Positive Views |
|---|---|
| talkative | friendly, chatty, articulate, vocal, communicative |
| hyperactive | busy, fast, quick, energized, motivated, lively |
| bossy | leadership skills, takes charge, organizer |
| stubborn | spunky, persistent, stick-to-it, never give up |
| dreamer | creative, artistic, resourceful, imaginative, inventive |
| impulsive | spontaneous, swift, hurried, speedy, fast mover |

## Empowering Messages

*Adult:* Becoming more aware of ADHD characteristics will help the child understand why she has certain problems learning and/or relating to others.

*Child:* ADHD traits can be negative or positive, depending upon how I respond to them.

# How Does It Feel?

## What the Experts Say

"Although a comprehensive treatment plan for ADHD may include behavior modification, cognitive therapy, family therapy, and training in social skills, stimulant medication is the mainstay of conventional treatment of ADHD." *

## Introducing the Concept

The more information a child with ADHD has about medication, the more actively she can participate in her own treatment. Medication might even make it possible for her to evaluate her own behavior and performance. Encourage the child to ask questions and share any concerns she may have about her medication.

## Let's Talk About It

1. Do you take medication to treat your ADHD?
2. How does the appropriate dosage of medication make you feel?
3. How do you feel when you don't take your medication?

## Empowering Activity

Ever wonder what a child feels like when she is on stimulant medication? Experts say that it is difficult to describe, but some relate the effects of the medication by using analogies. Share the following examples:

- It is like a filter. When people make jam, sometimes they use cheesecloth as a filter to separate the seeds and pulp from the juice. For some children with ADHD, taking medication is like filtering thoughts; just the important ones reach the brain; or
- It's like a funnel. It channels a flood of input and concentrates it into a stream; or
- It's like a lens. It takes the sun's light and focuses all of it on a small area, spotlighting only that which is important; or
- It's like a radio tuner. It eliminates the static of distractions so messages can be received on a clear frequency.

To convey the importance of filtering information, conduct an experiment.

*You will need:* Large and small plastic bowls, fine-meshed screen wire, sand, and gravel.
*Directions:*
1. Cut a piece of screen wire large enough to cover the top of the large bowl.
2. Mix the sand and gravel in the small bowl.
3. Have the child sprinkle a handful of sand and gravel on top of the screen wire.
4. Watch how the wire separates the sand from the gravel.
5. Explain that this is the way some medications filter out unneeded stimuli, thereby allowing a child to pay attention to the finer points.

## Empowering Messages

*Adult:* Using medication may not be right for every child, but for some it will be effective in helping the child filter out disruptive thoughts and sounds.

*Child:* Medication sometimes helps children with ADHD to function and perform better.

# It's in the Family

## What the Experts Say

Experts have recently proven that ADHD is hereditary. "About half the children with learning disabilities have family members with this disability." *

## Introducing the Concept

Studies of twins have determined that if one twin was ADHD, the other twin had an 80 to 90 percent chance of being ADHD, too. Making a child aware that ADHD runs in families helps remove the belief that she did something to cause the disorder and lets her know that there are probably family members who can relate to her.

## Let's Talk About It

1. Who in your family is very talkative?
2. Who in your family is impulsive?
3. Is anyone in your family considered a dreamer?
4. Is anyone in your family hyperactive?
5. Who in your family is easily distracted or has trouble focusing?
6. Has anyone in your family been diagnosed ADHD?

## Empowering Activity

If possible, ask an adult with ADHD to talk to the child about how he compensates for the disorder. Help the child identify specific family members with hyperactivity and/or attention deficit by completing a chart like the sample below.

***Directions:*** Include special notes of any ADHD characteristics next to the appropriate name. Make a family tree. Use the illustration as an example.

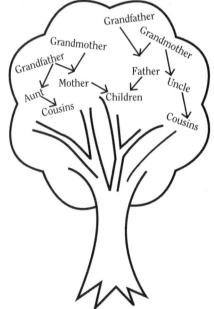

| NAME | CHARACTERISTICS |
|------|-----------------|
| Mom: | |
| Dad: | |
| Mom's mom: | |
| Dad's mom: | |
| Mom's dad: | |
| Dad's dad: | |
| Brothers: | |
| Sisters: | |
| Aunts: | |
| Uncles: | |
| Cousins: | |

## Empowering Messages

***Adult:*** ADHD is far more common in certain families than in the general population.

***Child:*** I can talk about my ADHD with people in my family, and they will understand.

# KEYS TO SUCCESS #2

## Glancing Back

The lessons and activities you have just completed with the child with ADHD were designed to help her understand important facts about ADHD. As reminders of what she has learned, have her complete the Keys to Understanding and Empowering Self-Talk found below.

## Keys to Understanding ADHD

Place these keys on the metal ring with the other keys to success.

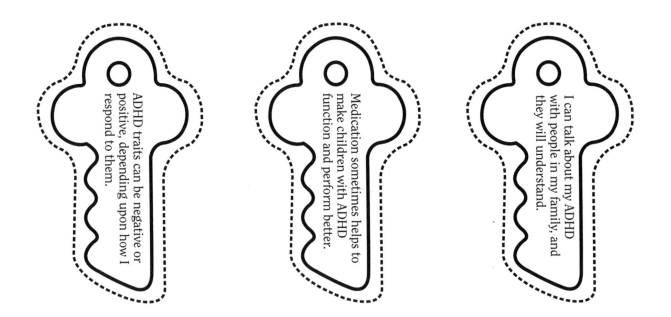

ADHD traits can be negative or positive, depending upon how I respond to them.

Medication sometimes helps to make children with ADHD function and perform better.

I can talk about my ADHD with people in my family, and they will understand.

## Empowering Self-Talk

Have the child copy and cut out the words below. Tell her to put the words in or near a framed photograph of a favorite family member who may have ADHD.

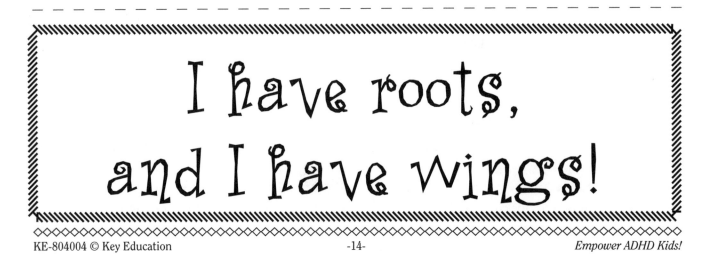

I have roots, and I have wings!

# Sugar and Spice It's Not

## What the Experts Say

In the past, refined sugar was said to cause increased hyperactivity in children with ADHD. Many recent studies have proven this false. A British study indicated: ".... only 16 percent of the hyperactive children tested reacted to sugar." *

## Introducing the Concept

Teaching good nutrition is one of the best ways to help children with ADHD stay healthy. A young child's healthy diet should include a variety of foods with plenty of grain products, vegetables, and fruits. It should be low in fat, saturated fat, and cholesterol. It should be moderate in sugars and salt. It should include enough calcium and iron to meet the child's nutritional requirements. It should not include a lot of fast food, soft drinks, high-calorie or high-fat snacks, or over-sized portions.

## Let's Talk About It

1. Do you eat healthy foods?
2. What is your favorite snack?
3. Do you think eating too much sugar causes ADHD?
4. Do you think a healthy diet will help you to feel better and give you the strength needed to deal with your ADHD?

## Empowering Activity

Often youngsters do not know if a snack is healthy or unhealthy. Help them distinguish between the two by playing a guessing game.

***Directions:*** One at a time, read the names of the snacks. The child is to put "thumbs up" for healthy snacks and a "thumbs down" for unhealthy snacks. Discuss the responses.

1. fatty, store-bought cookies
2. applesauce (unsweetened)
3. soda
4. bottled water
5. unsweetened dried cereal
6. snack cake
7. unsweetened fruit cup
8. cheddar sandwich crackers
9. low-fat or fat-free milk
10. candy bars
11. raisins/unsweetened dried fruit
12. sugary candies
13. 100% pure orange juice
14. sugary "fruit" drinks
15. peanuts
16. grapes
17. cheddar cheese
18. apple
19. potato chips
20. unbuttered popcorn

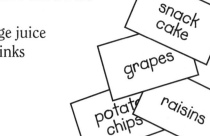

## Empowering Messages

*Adult:* When children maintain good nutrition, they will have the energy they need to cope with ADHD.

*Child:* Healthy choices in my diet will make me feel better and grow stronger.

# Eat Smart!

## What the Experts Say

"Links between diet and ADHD continue to be proposed, but at this point such claims cannot be taken seriously."* On the other hand, eating smart helps children with ADHD to feel better and gives them the energy to deal more effectively with their disorder.

## Introducing the Concept

Teaching children with ADHD about balanced nutrition will go a long way in teaching them to make better food choices and to remain healthy. Furthermore, since each person knows their body better than anyone else, each person should learn to monitor their own eating habits.

## Let's Talk About It

1. Do you like to eat? What are your favorite foods?
2. Do you know the basic food groups?
3. Have you ever used a Food Guide Pyramid?

## Empowering Activity

On the chalkboard or a large sheet of paper, draw a food pyramid. Explain each level.

1. The top level of the food pyramid includes fats, oils, and sweets. These foods are salad dressings and oils, cream, butter, margarine, sugars, soft drinks, candies, and sweet desserts. These foods provide calories and little nutrition. Use them sparingly.

2. The second level of the food pyramid includes milk, yogurt, and cheese. Proteins include beef, poultry, fish, nuts, and cheese. These foods give us protein, calcium, iron, and zinc.

3. The third level includes vegetables and fruits. We need to eat more of these foods for the vitamins, minerals, and fiber they supply.

4. At the bottom of the food pyramid are breads, cereals, rice, and pasta—all foods from grains. Children need many servings of these foods each day.

To reinforce balanced nutrition, for the next three days have the child chart her diet on a Food Guide Pyramid, found on page 17. Reproduce this page three times, one for each day the child is recording what she eats. For each serving the child eats, have her color an appropriate food in the designated level on the Food Guide Pyramid. At the end of three days, discuss the results. Does she need to eat more or less of certain foods?

## Empowering Messages

*Adult and child:* To stay healthy and feel good—eat smart!

# Charting My Diet – Day _____

Name _____

**Directions:** Find out if you are eating a balanced diet. For each serving you eat to-day, color an appropriate food in the designated level on the Food Guide Pyramid.

U.S. Department of Agriculture
Center for Nutrition Policy and Promotion

January 2000
Program Aid 1651

Adapted to reflect nutritional needs for elementary-aged children.

# It's a Distraction

## What the Experts Say

Children with ADHD are frequently called dreamers because they seem to live in another world. "Anything can distract them from the task at hand." *

## Introducing the Concept

Parents and teachers cannot always be aware of the things that distract a child. Only the child knows what makes it difficult for her to concentrate. For many of these children, noises are especially distracting. Designate quiet places where she can go when she needs to concentrate.

## Let's Talk About It

1. Can you work just as fast in a noisy room as in a quiet one?
2. If a person sitting behind you is drumming his pencil, does the tapping break your concentration?
3. If the TV is on in the room where you are reading, can you concentrate?
4. What kind of noises make it difficult for you to think?
5. If others are talking in the room, does that make it difficult for you to concentrate?

## Empowering Activity

Experiment to see if the child with ADHD can perform better without distractions by using the worksheets found on pages 19 and 20.

### Directions:

1. Time the child as she completes the puzzle on page 19. While she is working, try to distract her by playing loud music, walking around her, or tapping your pencil near her.
2. Now time her on the puzzle on page 20. This time eliminate all noises and distractions.
3. After correcting both tests, follow up with a discussion.

- How long did it take to complete Test A? _____

- How long did it take to complete Test B? _____

- How many did she get correct on Test A? _____

- How many did she get correct on Test B? _____

- Was there a big difference in her ability to concentrate when she didn't have noisy distractions?

## Empowering Messages

**Adult:** There are simple steps you can take to help children with ADHD increase their ability to perform tasks—one is to eliminate noisy distractions.

**Child:** When I need to concentrate, I will seek a quiet place.

# Test A

**Directions:** Write the answers on the lines.
1. What number between 1 and 35 is missing? _____
2. What number between 1 and 35 is listed two times? _____
3. What number between 1 and 35 is listed three times? _____

28    29    12    14    20

16    21    26

7    30    35    1    31

5    10    25    17

27    24    33    22    6    9

21    11    18    35

19    13    2    35    3

4    32    23    15    8

# Test B

**Directions:** Write the answers on the lines.
1. What number between 1 and 35 is missing? _____
2. What number between 1 and 35 is listed two times? _____
3. What number between 1 and 35 is listed three times? _____

15   7   27      17      24

30   33   9      32   1

23      14      26   2

12      19      34   25

21   3      35   16   29

8      12   4      17   31

18   5      20      6   11

28      17      22      13

# It's Not Caused by Schools

## What the Experts Say

Some teachers believe that small, well-structured classrooms will reduce the severity of ADHD symptoms. However, many parents believe ". . . . a more free-flowing classroom environment may allow them to learn more effectively, in their own way."*

## Introducing the Concept

ADHD is not caused by schools. A poorly structured or too-crowded classroom cannot give a child ADHD. However, a variety of factors do contribute to the student's ability to focus, including visual stimuli.

## Let's Talk About It

1. Do you find it difficult to concentrate when there are lots of things going on around you?
2. Can you think best in a private place rather than a crowded one?
3. What are some of the things that distract you in the classroom?
4. What are some of the things at home that distract you when you are trying to concentrate?

## Empowering Activity

Discuss the following examples as possible techniques for the child to improve her concentration in the classroom.

1. Would sitting near the teacher's desk or in the front row, where there are fewer distractions, make it easier to concentrate?
2. Would a peer tutor, giving you one-on-one help, make your learning easier?
3. Is sitting near a window, where there is traffic noise outside, or near a noisy heater or air conditioner distracting?
4. Would the use of a study carrel, work cubby, or an area where work can be done alone aid your progress? To insure privacy while the child works, help her create a study carrel.

***You will need:*** Three-section poster board display unit, paper, scissors, glue stick, and markers.

***Directions:*** Give the child time to draw pictures and write encouraging messages inside her carrel. Allow plenty of time for her to decorate it any way she wants. Make sure she is allowed to use it in class or at home whenever she needs to block out visual stimuli.

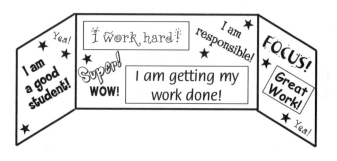

## Empowering Messages

***Adult:*** Only the child knows what steps can be taken to improve her concentration. Help her to identify distractions and discuss ways to eliminate them.

***Child:*** If I know what will improve my concentration and if I express it to my parents or teacher, they will help me.

◇◇◇◇◇◇◇◇◇◇◇◇◇◇◇◇◇◇◇◇◇◇◇◇◇◇◇◇◇◇◇◇◇◇◇◇◇◇◇◇◇◇◇◇◇◇◇

# KEYS TO SUCCESS #3

◇◇◇◇◇◇◇◇◇◇◇◇◇◇◇◇◇◇◇◇◇◇◇◇◇◇◇◇◇◇◇◇◇◇◇◇◇◇◇◇◇◇◇◇◇◇◇

## Glancing Back ---------------------------------------------------------------------------

The lessons and activities you have just completed with the child with ADHD were designed to help her cope more effectively with ADHD.

## Keys to Understanding ADHD -----------------------------------------------------

Place the new keys on the metal ring with the other keys to success.

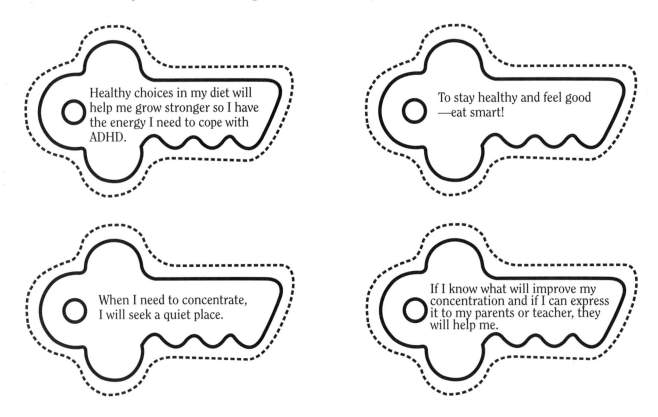

Healthy choices in my diet will help me grow stronger so I have the energy I need to cope with ADHD.

To stay healthy and feel good —eat smart!

When I need to concentrate, I will seek a quiet place.

If I know what will improve my concentration and if I can express it to my parents or teacher, they will help me.

## Empowering Self-Talk ----------------------------------------------------------------

Have the child copy and cut out the words below. Tell her to put the words on her bathroom mirror. Every morning while brushing her teeth, she can think the positive words over and over.

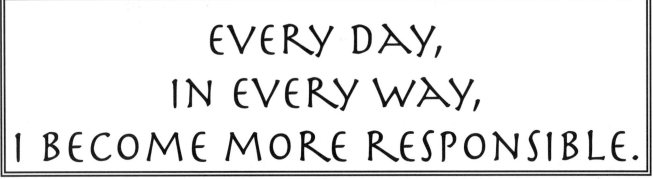

EVERY DAY,
IN EVERY WAY,
I BECOME MORE RESPONSIBLE.

◇◇◇◇◇◇◇◇◇◇◇◇◇◇◇◇◇◇◇◇◇◇◇◇◇◇◇◇◇◇◇◇◇◇◇◇◇◇◇◇◇◇◇◇◇◇◇

# CHAPTER TWO    I Must Champion Myself

## What the Experts Say

Life will be better and easier if the child learns how to take responsibility for managing her own ADHD. And since "ADHD is really more a collection of common features . . . in each child (or adult)," it will be up to the child to identify her own personal traits. *

## Introducing the Concept

To get through challenging situations, children with ADHD have to develop self-awareness so that they can control impulsiveness and focus their attention. Once children have developed this self-awareness, most children with ADHD become responsible problem-solvers.

## Let's Talk About It

To assist the child with ADHD in knowing which areas she may need to become self-aware, help her complete the following questionnaire.

1.  Do you dislike making changes? _____
2.  Are you easily distracted and find it difficult to focus your attention?_____
3.  Do you have difficulty planning ahead? _____
4.  Do you work best in a highly structured situation? _____
5.  Do you need more time than others to complete tasks?_____
6.  Do you often feel restless? _____
7.  Do you hurt people's feelings by speaking without thinking first? _____
8.  Are you sometimes reckless and do dangerous things? _____
9.  Do people say you fidget (drum fingers, kick leg, tap foot)?_____
10. Do you make snap decisions that end in disaster? _____
11. Do you over react to pressure?_____
12. Are you easily angered? _____
13. Do you make big deals out of unimportant things? _____
14. Do you often feel confused by what others want from you? _____
15. Do people say you talk too much? _____
16. Do people say you are moody? _____
17. Do you often forget things? _____
18. Do you have difficulty waiting your turn in line? _____
19. Do you have difficulty learning in the classroom setting? _____

## Empowering Activity

After identifying which specific traits the child has trouble with, help her make a list of personal concerns. *Example:*   1.  I am easily distracted and sometimes I find it difficult to focus.
2.  I sometimes forget things.
3.  Some people say I talk too much.

## Empowering Messages

*Adult:* There are many different characteristics of ADHD. Not all children demonstrate every trait. There may be only a few behavior traits that are of concern to each child.

*Child:* The more I learn about ADHD, the more empowered I become.

# What! Me? Overreact? Never!!!

## What the Experts Say

Sometimes children with ADHD are more easily angered than other children. "When angry . . . ADD children may produce fabulous temper tantrums." *

## Introducing the Concept

To the child with ADHD, not getting her way can seem like the end of the world. Even though a temper tantrum may last only a few minutes, it is genuinely disruptive to a parent or teacher. Every child with ADHD must learn that throwing a tantrum is an inappropriate way to deal with anger.

## Let's Talk About It

1. How do you feel when you don't get what you want—sad, angry, enraged?
2. What do you do when you don't get your own way?
3. Have you ever seen someone throw a temper tantrum?

## Empowering Activity

Some children with ADHD are emotionally as self-centered as toddlers. To convey the inappropriateness of temper tantrums, role-play a child not getting her way.

***Directions:*** Break into pairs. One person plays the parent, and the other plays the child. The child asks to go water skiing with a friend. The parent calmly explains that since the child does not know how to swim, she cannot go. The child tries to convince the parent to let her go and then overreacts by throwing a tantrum. If working with a small group, have each pair share its skit with the others. If working with an individual, tape-record the skit and replay it for the child. Afterward, discuss how tantrums are an overreaction to disappointment. Conclude by listing appropriate ways of dealing with frustration.

***Examples:***

- walk away until calmed down
- verbally express your feelings calmly and politely to a parent or teacher
- ask to do something else instead
- go someplace alone and do deep-breathing exercises
- go outside and shoot baskets
- find a quiet place and read a book

## Empowering Messages

***Adult:*** A child will not continue to throw temper tantrums in order to get what she wants if you never give in to the tantrums.

***Child:*** I can feel disappointed as long as I don't demonstrate my disappointment in inappropriate ways.

# My Own Architect

## What the Experts Say

"Some ADHD children may struggle, unable to move forward through critical stages of development." *

## Introducing the Concept

Most youngsters do not know which positive character traits they really want to embrace. You can help by offering a range of ideas.

## Let's Talk About It

1. Do you ever feel like you're stuck and don't know which way to go?
2. Do you ever worry so much about a decision that you don't take any action?
3. Is school work difficult for you because you run out of time?
4. What are some characteristics that will empower you as a child with ADHD?

## Empowering Activity

Explain how an architect plans a house before building begins. Ask, "Can you imagine what would happen if someone just built a house without a plan?" Say, "Building character is a bit like building a house. A person needs to know the attributes she wants to develop as her foundation." To find out what characteristics the child thinks she wants to develop, play the following game.

**Directions:** On individual index cards, write down the descriptive words listed below. Read each card to the child. Help her sort them into three piles: her character assets, traits she wants to develop, and traits she doesn't feel are important.

| | | | |
|---|---|---|---|
| loving | reliable | empathetic | patient |
| healthy | curious | cooperative | kind |
| polite | friendly | gentle | inquisitive |
| calm | problem solver | responsible | expressive |
| imaginative | adventurous | enjoys learning | generous |
| humorous | attentive | self-motivated | truthful |
| patient | honest | will ask for help | forgiving |
| grateful | flexible | good listener | empowered |
| learns from mistakes | | | |

On the back of the cards listing the traits she wants to develop, note practical ways she can master those characteristics. Give the child those cards to keep.

## Empowering Messages

**Adult:** When a child understands the traits that build character, she can take steps to build her own character.

**Child:** I am my own architect for building my own good character.

# Come About!

## What the Experts Say

Many ADHD kids do not adjust well to change. "Difficulty adjusting to changes in a routine often result from the excitement of doing something out of the ordinary." *

## Introducing the Concept

Imagine a large cruise ship suddenly receiving radio orders to return to the dock. It must slow down, turn in a wide circle, and then head back. Imagine how much energy that would take compared to moving along at its original speed and direction. It's about that difficult for a child with ADHD to change directions.

## Let's Talk About It

1. Do you dislike it when people change plans?
2. Do you sometimes dislike doing something, simply because you were not told about the plans ahead of time?

## Empowering Activity

It takes a great amount of energy to change directions. When someone asks a child with ADHD to make a quick turnabout, it may frustrate her. Say, "If sudden changes in plans make you feel frustrated, there is good reason." Explain to the child that it takes a great amount of energy to change directions. To demonstrate that changing directions is difficult, help the child create a miniature boat or raft.

*You will need:* Styrofoam meat tray, paper, paper or plastic straw, scissors, glue stick, and a tub of water.

### Directions:
1. Scrub the meat tray with soap and water.
2. Glue a paper sail to a toothpick and push it into the meat tray.
3. Fill the bathtub or a child's small wading pool with water.
4. By blowing on the boat or paddling the water around it, see how fast the child can get the boat from one side to the other.
5. Sailors call reversing the direction of a sail boat "coming about." Now have the child try coming about. Send the boat half way across the pool, and then make it come about to the starting place. Can it be done in the same amount of time it takes the boat to go straight across the water? Of course not!

## Empowering Messages

*Adult:* Acknowledging that a child's frustration is understandable will go a long way in making her feel better about herself.

*Child:* Changing directions can be frustrating, but if I slow down and think about it, I can be flexible.

◇◇◇◇◇◇◇◇◇◇◇◇◇◇◇◇◇◇◇◇◇◇◇◇◇◇◇◇◇◇◇◇◇◇◇◇◇◇◇◇◇◇◇◇◇◇◇◇◇◇◇◇◇◇◇◇◇◇◇◇◇◇◇◇

# Tools of the Trade

◇◇◇◇◇◇◇◇◇◇◇◇◇◇◇◇◇◇◇◇◇◇◇◇◇◇◇◇◇◇◇◇◇◇◇◇◇◇◇◇◇◇◇◇◇◇◇◇◇◇◇◇◇◇◇◇◇◇◇◇◇◇◇◇

## What the Experts Say

"Children with ADHD frequently experience significant challenges at school." * One of their main challenges is simply staying focused.

## Introducing the Concept

Some children need visual cues and special aids when learning. Do you encourage the child to use a bookmark or run her finger under the line she is reading? Although these kinds of practices were once frowned upon, they can be very helpful for the child with ADHD.

## Let's Talk About It

1. When you read, do you have trouble keeping your mind on the book?
2. When you read, do you ever read the same line over and over?
3. When you read, do you stop thinking about the words you are reading and just let your mind wander?

## Empowering Activity

Using markers can help a child to focus. To demonstrate, assist her in taking the test on page 28. *(Answer key is found on page 64.)*

### Directions:

1. Have the child count the cows and time her while she does so. Record her answer and the amount of time it took.

2. Cover the puzzle with a sheet of paper. Time her as she slowly slides the paper down and counts the cats. Record her answer and the amount of time it took.

3. Cover the page again. Time her as she slides the paper from left to right and counts the foxes. Record her answer and the amount of time it took.

4. Finally, time her as she uses a pencil to cross out each hippo as she counts it. Record her answer and the amount of time it took .

5. Check the answer key to see how accurate her counting was. Was she more accurate when using a paper to make lines or columns or when using a pencil to keep track?

6. Which did she count fastest: cows, cats, foxes, or hippos?

7. Which focusing method helped her the most? Did she do better moving her eyes across the page from left to right or did she do better scanning the page from top to bottom?

## Empowering Messages

*Adult:* Encourage the child with ADHD to find and use aids that will help her focus.
*Child:* I can devise tools that will help me focus my attention.

◇◇◇◇◇◇◇◇◇◇◇◇◇◇◇◇◇◇◇◇◇◇◇◇◇◇◇◇◇◇◇◇◇◇◇◇◇◇◇◇◇◇◇◇◇◇◇◇◇◇◇◇◇◇◇◇◇◇◇◇◇◇◇◇

# Focusing Puzzle

*Empower ADHD Kids!*

# A Child's Space

## What the Experts Say

Many children with ADHD do better in highly structured situations. Experts advise parents: "Make certain to provide your child with a quiet, uncluttered place to do homework, school projects, etc." *

## Introducing the Concept

Is the ADHD child's home and school work areas well-organized? Take a look at the space where she must concentrate. Is it conducive to developing good study habits? Talk to her to find out what she needs for a good study environment.

## Let's Talk About It

1. Do you have a comfortable chair where you sit and study?
2. Is there adequate lighting where you read?
3. Do you have the needed supplies for completing your school work?
4. Do you have the books you need to complete your assignments?
5. Is the area where you study a quiet place where you can work undisturbed?

## Empowering Activity

Talk to the child about what she needs to create a productive study center. Ask her to make a sketch of her ideal space. Have her list what she needs to make that space a reality. Invest some time (and money if necessary) in creating a space just for her. Consider and discuss the following:

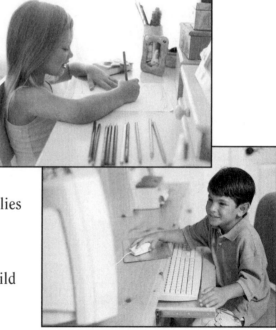

1. Carefully pick the spot where she should always go to study.
2. When choosing the spot, make sure it is quiet and free from distractions.
3. Clear the study area of all clutter.
4. Make sure the spot has proper lighting and comfortable furniture.
5. Provide all the materials needed to get organized (paper, pencils, pencil sharpener, erasers, ruler, tape, scissors, dictionary).
6. Provide a way of organizing the materials and supplies (desk drawers, work bins, pencil box).
7. Provide study materials such as index cards for creating flash cards.
8. Make sure the study area is not too warm so the child will not become drowsy.

## Empowering Messages

**Adult:** Remember, you couldn't do your job if you didn't have the proper facilities. Neither can the child with ADHD.

**Child:** Having a proper study space will help me become the kind of student I want to be.

# Snail's Pace or Cheetah's Speed?

## What the Experts Say

Some children with ADHD tend to work very slowly while others carelessly rush through their school work. Experts say: "An ADD child may have a poor sense of time and place." *

## Introducing the Concept

Most children with ADHD mean well. Children with ADHD cannot help it if they move at different speeds than others. They do not vary their speed to annoy others. A child with ADHD can be like a turtle or a cheetah. We don't expect turtles to speed up or cheetahs to slow down. If poor timing divides a child with ADHD from her family, teachers, and peers, her self-esteem may plummet. Be patient with her and let her know that her pace is acceptable to you.

## Let's Talk About It

1. Does it embarrass you if it takes you longer to do things than it takes others?
2. Do adults sometimes tell you that your work is messy or incomplete?
3. If you and a friend are silently reading on the same page and she finishes reading the page first, do you pretend to be done too?
4. Do you ever skip lines or pages so you can finish reading before others?

## Empowering Activity

To find out if the child is aware of her unique pace, ask her to pick the animal in each pair whose speed is most like her own.

## Empowering Messages

*Adult:* Animals move at different speeds; we don't think they are too slow or too fast. Don't resent the ADHD child's unique pace.

*Child:* When I am alone, my speed is exactly right for me. In a group, I will try to keep pace with the others.

# KEYS TO SUCCESS #4

## Glancing Back

The lessons and activities you have just completed with the child with ADHD were designed to help her identify some of the ways ADHD interferes with her learning.

## Keys to Understanding ADHD

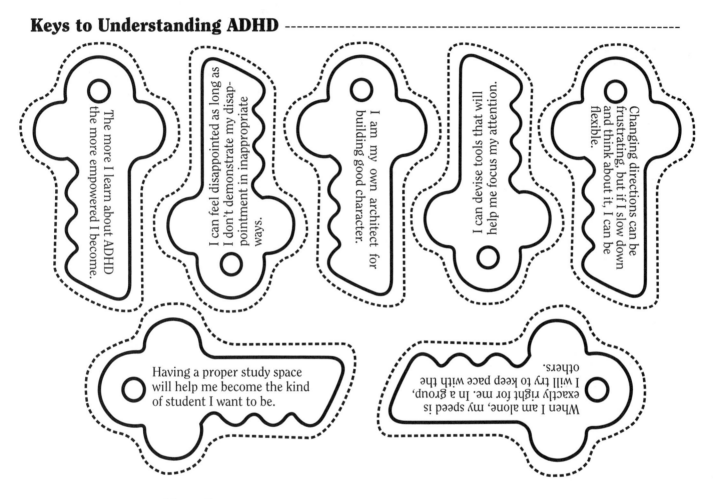

The more I learn about ADHD the more empowered I become.

I can feel disappointed as long as I don't demonstrate my disappointment in inappropriate ways.

I am my own architect for building good character.

I can devise tools that will help me focus my attention.

Changing directions can be frustrating, but if I slow down and think about it, I can be flexible.

Having a proper study space will help me become the kind of student I want to be.

When I am alone, my speed is exactly right for me. In a group, I will try to keep pace with the others.

## Empowering Self-Talk

Have the student copy and cut out the words below. Place the words on the bedroom light switch. Every night as she turns off the light, tell her to repeat the words five times.

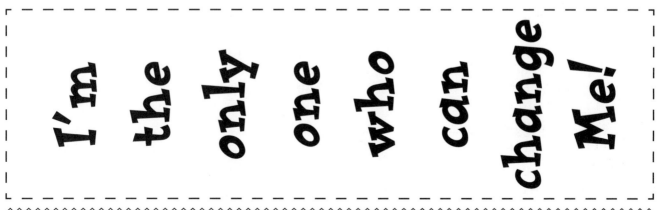

I'm the only one who can change Me!

# Try Some Exercise

## What the Experts Say

Children with ADHD sometimes have a great deal of excess energy. If the energy isn't used, they might display signs of hyperactivity such as fidgeting, squirming, running, climbing around, or talking excessively. "The goal is to channel excessive activity into acceptable activities." *

## Introducing the Concept

A child with ADHD has a special type of intensity, energy, and enthusiasm can enhance life for her and those around her. Focusing on this energy as a positive quality and having others to do so as well will greatly contribute to the child's self-esteem and academic success.

## Let's Talk About It

1. Do you think you have more energy than most children?
2. Do you think having a lot of energy is a good thing?
3. When you have to sit still but you feel like you want to jump around, what do you do?
4. Have you ever practiced sitting quietly for a few minutes?
5. Have you ever tried listening to soothing music to calm yourself?
6. Is exercise a part of your daily routine?
7. Do you know that exercise is a good way to utilize excess energy?

## Empowering Activity

Help the child see that excess energy can be channeled and used for enjoyable purposes. Explain that she can release excess energy and get exercise while participating in many different sports and activities.

### Directions:

1. Have her fold a large sheet of paper into four equal sections.
2. Read the list of physical activities found below.
3. In each section, ask her to draw a picture of one of the four activities she likes best.

- bicycling
- yoga, kick boxing, or karate
- aerobics
- jogging
- basketball, football, or soccer
- running around a track
- rope jumping or skate boarding
- playing follow-the-leader or tag
- dog walking

- roller blading or ice skating
- working out at a gym
- playing the drums
- mile-long walk
- skiing or snow boarding
- camping
- dance lessons
- hiking
- jumping jacks

## Empowering Messages

**Adult:** While the child with ADHD is confined to a classroom, excess energy not only makes learning difficult, it can further erode her self-confidence.

**Child:** If I learn to channel my extra energy, having it will become a positive in my life.

# Stop, Wait, and Think

## What the Experts Say

"There are tremendous variations in the behaviors, personalities, and characteristics of children who fall under the one diagnostic umbrella of ADHD."* For most children with ADHD, consistently making good decisions or using effective judgment is extremely difficult.

## Introducing the Concept

In the ADHD child's hurry-up world, it probably feels uncomfortable to be idle. But to change poor decision-making patterns, the child must be taught to stop and think before she acts.

## Let's Talk About It

1   Do you sometimes make unwise decisions?
2.  Are your snap decisions usually wrong ones?
3.  Have you ever looked back on something and wished that you had done it differently or not at all?

## Empowering Activity

Discuss how the judges on television courtrooms weigh the evidence on both sides and listen to both parties before making a judgment. Say, "Being able to show good judgment is not a gift that all people possess. When faced with an important decision, making a list of pros and cons sometimes helps people think more clearly."

### Directions:

1.  Leaving out what's in parentheses, read one of the decisions listed below.
2.  Without giving the child time to think about it, have her make a snap decision.
3.  Discuss the decision and make a list of pros and cons for her decision.
4.  Next, read the part of the question that is in parentheses and make a new list of pros and cons. Were her snap decisions good ones?

### Decisions:

1. You forgot your money, so you didn't get to buy lunch. You arrive home from school famished and find a delicious cake on the kitchen table. Do you cut yourself a piece? *(The cake was for your dad's birthday party; there's no time to bake another.)*

2. You need money to go with friends to the amusement park after school. You find a five-dollar bill on the playground. Do you turn it in or keep it? *(The next day at school, a friend with tears in her eyes, tells you that yesterday she lost five dollars that her father had given her to buy flowers for her sick mother.)*

## Empowering Messages

*Adult:* Show children with ADHD how to weigh the pros and cons of a choice before making decisions.

*Child:* Before I make decisions, I give myself permission to stop, wait, and think.

# A Very Long List

## What the Experts Say

"ADHD children are not just forgetful—they are amazingly forgetful. They lose track of time and frequently lose things." * To help, experts advise parents to provide their children with written lists.

## Introducing the Concept

Most adults have developed techniques to help them remember things, such as asking others to remind them, using date books, and making lists. Keep in mind that it is even more difficult for children with ADHD to remember. Encourage them to develop the habit of making lists.

## Let's Talk About It

1. Do you sometimes forget things?
2. What kinds of things do you forget?
3. Have you ever seen a shopper at the supermarket looking at a list?
4. How does your mother remember special dates?
5. How does your father remember business appointments?

## Empowering Activity

Help the child realize that getting organized will give her freedom and flexibility to handle unanticipated events, time to savor friendships, and the feeling of accomplishment. Say, "There is a lot to remember. Forgetting is understandable because you have so many things on your mind. Making lists is an excellent way to keep track of things." Encourage the child to use lists by making a very long list together. See how many memory cues you and the child can list.

### Directions:

1. Begin by cutting a two- to three-foot-long piece of shelf paper or butcher paper. (The length of the paper is for drama.)
2. Write very large so that you will use the whole length of the paper and make a list of "Ways to Remember."

### Examples:

- Write on a self-stick note and put it where I will see it.
- Use a personal chalkboard for messages to myself.
- Tie a string around my finger.
- Ask someone to remind me.
- Write important events on a calendar.

WAYS TO REMEMBER

- Write it on a Post-It™ and put it where I will see it.
- Use a personal chalkboard for messages to myself.
- Tie a string around my finger.
- Ask someone to remind me.
- Write important events on a calendar.

When the list is as long as you both can make it, ask the child to pick her favorites. Let the child quiz you to see how many of the ideas you can remember.

## Empowering Messages

**Adult:** Be a model of organization by posting lists, recording events on a calendar, and using other memory cues.

**Child:** Being organized so that I don't forget things will help me get everything done on time.

# At the End of the Line

## What the Experts Say

Some children with ADHD are impulsive and have difficulty waiting, especially waiting in long lines. Children have not lived long enough or had enough experience to know: "Patience is learned with personal success and by satisfaction with our accomplishments." *

## Introducing the Concept

Most people do not enjoy standing in line. For a child with ADHD it can be extremely unnerving, even painful. Learning to wait in a long line is a difficult skill to master, especially for children with ADHD.

## Let's Talk About It

1.  Do you dislike waiting in lines?
2.  How do you feel when you have to get into a long line?
3.  Do you ever bully your way to the front of the line?
4.  Do you ever take cuts from someone in the middle of the line?
5.  Do you go to the end of the line but complain while you are standing there?
6.  When you see people in line in front of you, do you feel like they have beaten you in a race?

## Empowering Activity

Some children with ADHD would rather miss an exciting activity than stand in line to wait for their turn. Ask, "Have you ever skipped doing something you wanted to do just because it required standing in a line?" Ask, "What if sport games had no rules? Chaos would rule. Right?"

Demonstrate how important lines are by having the child draw pictures of the scenarios listed below. On separate occasions have her illustrate one from each category.

### Directions:
**1. Chaos in Sports:**
- football players standing anywhere they want during the kick off
- basketball players making baskets in both baskets
- baseball players running the bases in all directions

**2. Chaos in the Market Place:**
- no supermarket aisles—food is in one huge pile
- no lines at the store—customers push and shove to check out
- restaurant waiters wait on people in random order

**3. Chaos at School:**
- no cafeteria line—kids shove and push to get in
- no school bus lines—kids rush to get on before the bus stops and squeeze in
- teachers do not call on students—those who shout the loudest get attention

## Empowering Messages

*Adult:* Your patience with the child will be mirrored in her patience with the world.

*Child:* Mastering patience will empower me.

# Ho-Hum, I'm Bored!

## What the Experts Say

Many children with ADHD have a tendency to get bored quickly. Some experts call children with ADHD "stimulation seekers." *

## Introducing the Concept

No one likes to be bored; however, boredom is something for which we each must hold ourselves accountable. Helping children with ADHD to see that their boredom is their responsibility and that they can make alternative choices will help empower them.

## Let's Talk About It

1. What do you do when you are bored?
2. How does it feel to be bored?
3. When you get bored, who is responsible?
4. What is the most exciting profession?
5. If you could spend a week doing anything, what would you do?

## Empowering Activity

Point out to the child that everyone gets bored once in a while. Ask, "Do you think that people with exciting jobs like a circus fire-eater or tightrope walker ever get bored? What about famous movie stars? Do you think they get bored making movies? Whose choice is it to remain bored?" Say, "If you choose not to be bored, there are many things that you can do to have fun."

To help the child become more responsible for her own entertainment, use the contract on page 37.

***Directions:*** Give the contract to the child. Begin by reading the activities listed at the top. Brainstorm ten more activities that she would find especially stimulating. Add those to the contract. Have the child fill out the contract and sign it. Encourage her to keep it and use it whenever she gets bored.

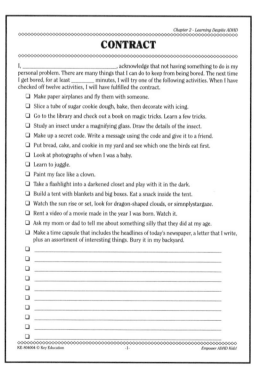

## Empowering Messages

***Adult:*** Help the child see that boredom is an opportunity to do something new.

***Child:*** When I get bored, that's my opportunity to choose an exciting activity.

◇◇◇◇◇◇◇◇◇◇◇◇◇◇◇◇◇◇◇◇◇◇◇◇◇◇◇◇◇◇◇◇◇◇◇◇◇◇◇◇◇◇◇◇◇◇◇◇◇◇◇◇◇◇◇◇◇◇◇◇◇◇

# CONTRACT

◇◇◇◇◇◇◇◇◇◇◇◇◇◇◇◇◇◇◇◇◇◇◇◇◇◇◇◇◇◇◇◇◇◇◇◇◇◇◇◇◇◇◇◇◇◇◇◇◇◇◇◇◇◇◇◇◇◇◇◇◇◇

I, _____, acknowledge that not having something to do is my personal problem. There are many things that I can do to keep from being bored. The next time I get bored, for at least _____ minutes, I will try one of the following activities. When I have checked off 12 activities, I will have fulfilled the contract.

- ❏ Make paper airplanes and fly them with someone.
- ❏ Slice a tube of sugar-cookie dough, bake, and then decorate the cookies.
- ❏ Go to the library and check out a book on magic tricks. Learn a few tricks.
- ❏ Study an insect under a magnifying glass. Draw the details of the insect.
- ❏ Make up a secret code. Write a message using the code and give it to a friend.
- ❏ Put bread, cake, and cookies in my yard and see which one the birds eat first.
- ❏ Look at photographs of me as a baby.
- ❏ Learn to juggle.
- ❏ Paint my face like a clown.
- ❏ Take a flashlight into a darkened closet and play with it in the dark.
- ❏ Build a tent with blankets and big boxes. Eat a snack inside the tent.
- ❏ Watch the sun rise or set, look for dragon-shaped clouds, or simply stargaze.
- ❏ Rent a video of a movie made in the year I was born. Watch it.
- ❏ Ask my mom or dad to tell me about something silly that they did at my age.
- ❏ Make a time capsule that includes the headlines from today's newspaper, a letter that I write, plus an assortment of interesting things. Bury the capsule in my backyard.

- ❏ _____
- ❏ _____
- ❏ _____
- ❏ _____
- ❏ _____
- ❏ _____
- ❏ _____
- ❏ _____
- ❏ _____
- ❏ _____

◇◇◇◇◇◇◇◇◇◇◇◇◇◇◇◇◇◇◇◇◇◇◇◇◇◇◇◇◇◇◇◇◇◇◇◇◇◇◇◇◇◇◇◇◇◇◇◇◇◇◇◇◇◇◇◇◇◇◇◇◇◇

# KEYS TO SUCCESS #5

## Glancing Back

The lessons and activities you have just completed with your child with ADHD were designed to help her recognize ways she can be responsible for her own happiness.

## Keys to Understanding ADHD

If I learn to channel my extra energy, having it will be a positive in my life.

Before I make decisions, I will give myself permission to stop, wait, and think.

Being organized, so that I don't forget things, will help me get everything done on time.

When I get bored, that's my opportunity to choose an exciting activity.

Mastering patience will help empower me.

## Empowering Self-Talk

Have the child copy and cut out the words listed to the right. Tell her to put the words on her desk as a reminder to take responsibility for her own learning.

Learning self-discipline will give me a strong sense of pride.

# CHAPTER THREE        All in a H.U.F.F.

## What the Experts Say

Many children with ADHD overreact when they are under pressure. One extreme way some over react is to strike out at others. It is paramount that children with ADHD learn how to "handle conflict without resorting to fighting." * "Parents nearly always comment on how their child with ADD tends to overreact. On the positive side, parents enjoy their child's enthusiasm when the overreaction is on the joyous side." **

## Introducing the Concept

Guide the child in understanding that anger isn't a bad thing; it signals us when something is wrong. Let the child know that all people get angry, but that it's how we react to anger that can get us into trouble and make us feel powerless. Explain that you will help the child learn how to deal with anger in socially acceptable ways.

## Let's Talk About It

1. Do you sometimes overreact?
2. What makes you the angriest?
3. What do you do when you get angry?

## Empowering Activity

Experts believe anger is a combination of hurt, being treated unfairly, fear, and frustration. Ask, "Remember the story of the three little pigs? The wolf huffed and puffed with anger." Say, "If you can remember that story, especially the HUFF, you will be able to better understand your anger."

***Directions:*** Write the anger acronym: H.U.F.F. on a card for the child to keep.

## H = Hurt   U = Unfairness   F = Fear   F = Frustration

Help the child see past the anger and identify her feelings with the following discussion questions:
1. You studied a long time for a test, but didn't pass. Are you angry or frustrated?
2. You are called to the chalkboard to solve a math problem that you don't understand. Are you angry or fearful?
3. You are not invited to a party, but most of your friends are invited. Are you angry, or do you feel hurt?
4. Your shoelace comes untied during a foot race; it slows you down and you lose. Are you angry, or do you feel the race was unfair?
5. Your mom picks you up from school half an hour late. Are you angry or hurt?
6. Your sister gets new shoes. You don't. Are you angry, or do you feel life is just unfair?

## Empowering Messages

***Adult:*** Teaching the child to identify underlying feelings is the beginning of successfully solving problems and resolving conflicts.

***Child:*** When I get angry, I will try to identify my true feelings: hurt, unfairness, fear, or frustration.

# Go Away Anger

## What the Experts Say

Sometimes children with ADHD have difficulty dealing with anger (hurt, unfairness, fear, frustration) in appropriate and socially acceptable ways: ("e.g., compromise, walk away from the situation, talk with an adult about the problem, etc.") *

## Introducing the Concept

Explain that anger isn't the problem; everyone gets angry. The problem is how we deal appropriately with strong, heated emotions.

## Let's Talk About It

1. Do you know the difference between hurt, unfairness, fear, and frustration?
2. Tell about a time when you felt cheated.
3. What is the scariest thing you can think of?
4. What is the most frustrating experience that you can recall?
5. Can you name a time when you felt hurt?

## Empowering Activity

Assisting the child in identifying underlying feelings behind anger will make it possible for her to deal with her feelings in socially acceptable ways. Say, "Some children believe that being angry is a bad thing. It isn't wrong to feel angry; all people get angry sometimes." Ask, "Would you like to learn some ways to make your anger *(hurt, unfairness, fear, frustration)* easier to deal with?"

Experiment with the calming techniques listed below to see which ones work best for her.

### Calming Exercises:

1. Lie on a big pillow or bed and close your eyes. Pretend that you are a cloud floating in the sky.
2. Stand tall and straight. Use your arms and hands to make believe that you are a flower budding and then blooming.
3. Crouch down and then slowly rise, pretending to be the sun coming up above a mountain. Then slowly reverse the movement, pretending you are the setting sun.
4. Take a flashlight into a darkened closet and lie on the floor. Use the beam of light to make dancing designs on the ceiling and walls.
5. Sit with your eyes closed. Use your fingertips to massage your forehead, temples, and scalp.
6. Close your eyes. Pretend you are a helium balloon rising high above the earth and slowly, ever so slowly, drifting away from all your worries.
7. Practice deep-breathing and relaxation exercises by counting to five and slowly releasing your breath. Repeat this seven times.
8. Do simple and relaxing stretches on the floor.

## Empowering Messages

*Adult:* Teaching a child to deal effectively with her anger will keep her from responding in an inappropriate manner.

*Child:* When I feel anger, hurt, unfairness, fear, or frustration, I can relax with a calming exercise.

# Molehills or Mountains

## What the Experts Say

"An odd but interesting quality that often accompanies Attention Deficit Disorder is an intensity of feeling that often goes way beyond normal." *

## Introducing the Concept

Children with ADHD sometimes turn little things into big things. Over-responding can escalate problems that might be solved by simply looking at the situation from another perspective. Learning to look at things in a variety of ways is a great skill. Children who master this skill are happier and grow up to be valued employees, spouses, and parents.

## Let's Talk About It

1. What do you think it means when people say: "Someone is making a mountain out of a molehill?"
2. What kind of things really bother you?
3. Who is it that can make you angry very quickly?
4. Which tasks frustrate you the most?

## Empowering Activity

Provide opportunities for the child to look at things from different perspectives. On separate occasions, encourage her to complete each of the experiments listed below.

### Directions:

1. How does the world look to a baby before he learns to walk? Have the child crawl around on her hands and knees. Tell her to look up from under the tables, beds, and furniture in the house or classroom. Have a conversation with her while she is on her knees. Ask, "How do adults look different from this angle?"
2. Get a magnifying glass and watch ants working. Try to follow one particular ant around for a while. Ask, "How busy is it? Do ants seem to communicate? Do they ever stop working?" Explain that ants are too busy working to play, to sleep, or to get angry.
3. Take the child to the tallest building in your city. Ride an elevator to the top floor. Look out at the city. Ask, "Do people seem smaller? Do your problems seem smaller, too?"
4. Buy rose-colored glasses or use pink cellophane to make a pane. Tape cellophane to regular glasses or sunglasses. For an hour, have the child walk around viewing a rose-colored world. Ask, "How does this affect your spirit? Do you feel happier?"
5. Help the child list five things she worried about the most a year ago. Ask, "Do these things still bother you? Were your worries needless?"

## Empowering Messages

*Adult:* People choose to be negative or positive. Help the child with ADHD to become a more positive person.

*Child:* How I look at things can make a big difference in my attitude.

# Stop and Think

## What the Experts Say

Children with ADHD have a tendency to speak spontaneously. "Impulsive behavior is usually described as being unable to or finding it difficult to stop to reflect before speaking or acting." *

## Introducing the Concept

You can teach a child with ADHD to phrase things in a way that will get her point across without hurting someone's feelings. This may take some practice, but if the child is to have friends and be a positive part of her family, learning to be polite is a vital skill.

## Let's Talk About It

1. Have you ever heard the old saying "Sticks and stones may break my bones, but words will never hurt me?" What do you think this means?
2. Do you think words can hurt people?
3. When was it that someone's words hurt you?
4. Do you sometimes say things without thinking about how it might hurt someone's feelings?

## Empowering Activity

For a child with ADHD, telling the truth usually means blurting out the first thing that comes into her head. Without thoughts of malice, the child often hurts others. Being prepared is the first step in learning appropriate communication skills. Use the questions below to rehearse polite responses to situations which ordinarily might bring out the worst in her.

### Sticky Situations:

1. An unpopular child in your class invites you to come play at his house. How could you politely decline?
2. A girl in your class asks if you like her new dress. You do not think it is very special. How will you answer her in a polite way?
3. You are spending the night with a friend. The friend's mother serves liver and onions, which you hate. What will you do or say?
4. Your sister and her friends are watching TV. You don't like what they are watching. What will you do or say?
5. Your grandmother knits you a pea-green-and-orange striped sweater. It is fuzzy and really ugly. She tells you to wear it to a party. What will you do and say?
6. Your baseball team is going out for pizza after the game. Since your team won, your mom wants to take you out for a hamburger to celebrate. You would rather be with the team. What will you say to your mother?
7. A boy unjustly accuses you of taking his pencil. What will you say to him?

## Empowering Messages

**Adult:** Being polite is easier if the child has an opportunity to think things through in advance.
**Child:** If I stop and think, in any situation, I can respond in a polite way.

# Consequences and Lessons

## What the Experts Say

"Because of their impulsiveness, children with ADD are less likely to think before acting. They act before considering the consequences." *

## Introducing the Concept

Everyone has to make decisions, but decision-making without thinking through the consequences can be disastrous. For a child with ADHD, learning from mistakes is sometimes the best way to learn. When the child makes a mistake, take the time to discuss what happened and encourage her to verbalize what she learned from the experience.

## Let's Talk About It

1. Do you like to make decisions?
2. What is the most difficult decision you have ever had to make?
3. Do you like to make mistakes?
4. When you make a mistake, how does it make you feel?
5. How do you feel when you make a decision that turns out well?

## Empowering Activity

Learning from mistakes can only happen when consequences occur. Use the events listed below to help the child see the lessons learned from accepting consequences. After each statement, ask two questions: "What might be the consequences? What might be learned from the mistake?"

### Consequences and Lessons:

1. You stay up late watching TV instead of studying your spelling words.
2. You pack only candy in your lunch pail.
3. A little kid is pushed in line and accidentally falls into you. Before you realize how small he is, you turn and hit him.
4. Without asking permission, you borrow your father's saw to trim a tree.
5. You ignore your mom when she tells you to wear your coat to school. It rains that day.
6. You pretend to be sick so you can stay home from school.
7. Your mom tells you to feed the dog before you go to school, but you forget.
8. You lose your house key and have to crawl inside through a tiny window.
9. Your teacher tells the class there might be a pop quiz. You don't study because you think she is bluffing. She wasn't!
10. You tease your sister and make her cry.

## Empowering Messages

*Adult:* When the child with ADHD makes a poor decision, she needs to accept the consequences and learn from the experience.

*Child:* If I learn from my mistakes, my mistakes become important teachers.

# KEYS TO SUCCESS #6

## Glancing Back ----------------------------------------------------------------

The lessons and activities you have just completed with your child with ADHD were designed to help her understand how ADHD interferes with her relationships with others.

## Keys to Understanding ADHD -----------------------------------------------

When I get angry, I will try to identify my feelings of hurt, unfairness, fear, or frustration, and do some calming exercises.

How I look at things can make a big difference.

If I stop and think, in any situation, I can respond in a polite way.

If I learn from my mistakes, my mistakes can become important teachers.

## Empowering Self-Talk -------------------------------------------------------

Have the child copy and cut out the words below. Tell her to hang the words in a quiet, secret place like her closet or a spot in the basement where she can go when she wants to get calm.

# Stop and think!
# I can look at things through a positive light!

# C.L.O.W.N. Around

## What the Experts Say

Children with ADHD often interrupt others when they are speaking and generally do not have very good listening skills. When giving instructions to children with ADHD, experts recommend: "Stop at various points in a conversation to check for understanding of what is being discussed." *

## Introducing the Concept

Being a good listener is one of the most important social skills a person can acquire. If you can teach the child some simple listening techniques, others will value conversations with her, her relationships will improve, and she will win new friends.

## Let's Talk About It

1. Do you ever interrupt others while they are talking?
2. Do you often forget what others have just said?
3. Do you think that what others have to say is usually boring?
4. Are you a good listener? Would you like to be a better listener?

## Empowering Activity

The child's listening skills will greatly improve if you teach her the following five easy steps to good listening. Say, "When you carefully listen to another person, you demonstrate that you care about their thoughts. Today you are going to be learning five easy steps to becoming a good listener."

***Directions:*** Begin by reading the five steps and sharing the action for each line. Help her memorize the steps by using the motions.

---

**C**lose your lips — index finger to pursed lips

**L**ook at the speaker — point to both eyes

**O**pen your mind — cup both ears.

**W**ait to speak — put fingertips over lips.

**N**od your head — nod head.

---

## Empowering Messages

***Adult:*** Model good listening for the child with ADHD by following the five steps yourself.
***Child:*** Good listeners are sought after friends, quick learners, and empowered people.

# Nobody's Perfect

## What the Experts Say

Since children with ADHD have trouble learning, they often have poor self-esteem and are critical of themselves. Encourage the child to refrain from comparing her performance to others. Teach her that personal improvements are her only contest. "Failure is an inhibitor. Success is a motivator." *

## Introducing the Concept

Sometimes children with ADHD call themselves names like stupid, bad, or loser. It's counterproductive when children say mean things to themselves. Keep reminding the child that no one is perfect. The nature of being human makes it impossible to be perfect. Remind the child that when she makes a mistake, it is her opportunity to learn. Teach her to turn the lessons she learns from mistakes into positive statements about herself. ***Example:*** I failed my spelling test because I didn't study, but I will study next week and I will pass that test.

## Let's Talk About It

1. Is anyone ever perfect?
2. Do you sometimes think that you are dumb?
3. Do you often think you could have done better?
4. When you learn from your mistakes, what does that make you?

## Empowering Activity

Help the child reprogram negativity. Becoming aware of the counterproductive habit is the first step in changing her attitude about herself. Say, "Every time you think something negative about yourself or call yourself a bad name, I want you to stop!" Ask, "Do you think you can do that?" Say, "When you make a mistake, instead of saying something mean to yourself, tell yourself what you have learned from the experience." Practice rethinking and rephrasing words using the examples listed below.

***Directions:*** Read each sentence. The child is to rephrase each sentence in a positive statement.
1. You forgot to take a pencil to school. Instead of saying, "Boy, that was really stupid," you could say, "Anyone can forget to bring a pencil. Today I will ask my friend if I can borrow one from her. Tomorrow I will remember to bring my pencil."
2. You didn't study for a math test, and you failed the test. Instead of telling yourself you are terrible at math, you could say . . . .
3. You lose your temper and yell at your best friend. Instead of telling yourself that you are mean or a bad person, you could say . . . .
4. Your mother asks you to turn down your radio. You slam your bedroom door as loudly as you can. Instead of pouting and thinking how much you hate yourself (or your mother), you could say . . . .

## Empowering Messages

***Adult:*** We program ourselves with our own positive or negative thoughts.
***Child:*** If I have positive thoughts about myself, I will know I am terrific, and I will become empowered.

# Rules and Consequences

## What the Experts Say

Children with ADHD are often confused because they do not understand the rules or the consequences of breaking the rules. They often become completely frustrated when asked to explain certain actions or misbehaviors. Rules should be understood completely by the child. Furthermore, ". . . rules should be consistent and followed by everyone . . . ." *

## Introducing the Concept

Does the child with ADHD understand the basic rules of your home or classroom? Is she clear about what is expected of her and what will happen if she does not comply with the rules?

## Let's Talk About It

1. What is a rule?
2. What are some of the rules you must obey?
3. Can you give me an example of an unfair rule?
4. Can you name a fair rule?
5. Why are rules important?

## Empowering Activity

To find out if the child understands rules and consequences, have her verbalize three rules and the consequences of breaking each rule.

***Directions:*** List three basic rules that she must follow. Record the consequence of breaking the rules and whether she believes the consequences to be fair or unfair. Talk about the consequences that she believes are unfair. Try to mutually agree upon new consequences for the rules which she sees as unfair.

**Rule:** _____

**Consequence:** _____

**Fair/Unfair:** _____

**Rule:** _____

**Consequence:** _____

**Fair/Unfair:** _____

**Rule:** _____

**Consequence:** _____

**Fair/Unfair:** _____

## Empowering Messages

***Adult:*** Children should not be held accountable for things they don't understand.

***Child:*** When I accept the consequences for my misbehavior and learn from the experience, I am empowering myself.

# Time-Ins

## What the Experts Say

For older children with ADHD, time-out is often an effective consequence for misbehavior. But the time-out method of behavior modification isn't as effective when working with younger children with ADHD. "Their anger escalates when they are sent to another room for a time-out, and they become resentful at being sent away. Time-out reinforces all the negative messages they are accustomed to receiving about themselves." *

## Introducing the Concept

There is a better method of holding a young child accountable without isolating her: time-ins. A time-in chair is placed in the same room as the parent or teacher. The child must remain there and be silent for a given time. This gives her time to reflect about the problem and figure out a more appropriate response. It makes her, not the parent or teacher, responsible for solving the problem.

## Let's Talk About It

1. What does it mean to take time-out?
2. When you misbehave, are you told to take time-out?
3. Does being sent to a place where you are alone help you gain control, or does it make you even angrier?
4. Have you ever heard of time-ins?
5. If you are being disciplined, would you rather have time to think about it alone or would you prefer to remain in the same room with others?
6. Do you think young children should be held responsible for solving some of their own problems?

## Empowering Activity

Many children believe that to discipline means to punish. Explain that to discipline actually means to teach. When the child with ADHD needs to be disciplined *(taught)*, how does she wish to be handled? Find out by discussing it with the child. Use the questions listed below as guides.

1. What disciplinary action do you believe would help you to learn more quickly?
2. Can you think of a good reason why time-ins, instead of time-outs, should be used?
3. Do you think time-outs or time-ins would be the best discipline for you? Why?

## Empowering Messages

*Adult:* If the form of discipline you are using isn't helping the child learn, maybe there is another method that will work more effectively for her.

*Child:* Only I know what method will speed up my learning; I will tell my parents or teacher what works best for me.

# KEYS TO SUCCESS #7

## Glancing Back

The lessons and activities you have just completed with your child with ADHD were designed to help her understand some of the ways ADHD interferes with her social and emotional stability.

## Keys to Understanding ADHD

Good listeners are sought after friends, quick learners, and empowered people.

If I have positive thoughts about me, I will know I am terrific, and I will become empowered.

When I accept the consequences for misbehavior and learn from the experience, I am empowering myself.

Only I know what method will accelerate my learning; I will tell my parents or teacher what works best for me.

When I can clearly state my ideas and needs, I magnify my empowerment.

## Empowering Self-Talk

Have the student copy and cut out the words listed to the right. Tell her to put them by the telephone. While she is talking on the telephone she can read the words.

◇◇◇◇◇◇◇◇◇◇◇◇◇◇◇◇◇◇◇◇◇◇◇◇◇◇◇◇◇◇◇◇◇◇◇◇◇◇◇◇◇◇◇◇◇◇◇◇◇◇◇◇◇◇◇◇◇◇◇◇◇◇◇◇

# CHAPTER FOUR                    Excel!

◇◇◇◇◇◇◇◇◇◇◇◇◇◇◇◇◇◇◇◇◇◇◇◇◇◇◇◇◇◇◇◇◇◇◇◇◇◇◇◇◇◇◇◇◇◇◇◇◇◇◇◇◇◇◇◇◇◇◇◇◇◇◇◇

## What the Experts Say

"The more fully a child with ADHD can begin to understand and take ownership of her challenges... the more successful she may become at self-management and the higher her self-esteem is likely to be." *

## Introducing the Concept

Children with ADHD often have above average IQs and many have extremely high IQs. To celebrate these gifts, children must be aware of the areas where they excel.

## Let's Talk About It

1. What does it mean to excel?
2. What are some of your talents?
3. What are some gifts you have that many others do not have?

## Empowering Activity

Some ADHD characteristics are extremely positive, but if kids do not recognize their strong points, they cannot celebrate them. Help the child discover which of the positive ADHD characteristics are part of her personality. Ask, "Would you like to explore some of the ways in which you excel?"

*Directions:* Complete the following questionnaire with the child. When finished, make a list of her positive attributes. Give her the list to keep.

1. Do people often tell you that you are creative? _____
2. Are you artistic? _____
3. Are you friendly? Do you enjoy meeting new people? _____
4. Do you especially enjoy being told when you do a job well?_____
5. When you take time to do your schoolwork, do you get good marks?_____
6. When you decide to do something, can you think of a variety of ways to do it? _____
7. Do your friends come to you for ideas and for ways to solve problems? _____
8. Are you funny and do people often laugh at the comical things you say or do? _____
9. Do people tell you that you have a charming personality? _____
10. Do you have good communication skills and can you talk your way out of most situations? ___

---

## Empowering Messages

*Adult:* Although many children with ADHD have difficulties in learning, a high percentage of them are intellectually gifted.

*Child:* Along with the challenging characteristics of ADHD, there are some good traits that can benefit me.

◇◇◇◇◇◇◇◇◇◇◇◇◇◇◇◇◇◇◇◇◇◇◇◇◇◇◇◇◇◇◇◇◇◇◇◇◇◇◇◇◇◇◇◇◇◇◇◇◇◇◇◇◇◇◇◇◇◇◇◇◇◇◇◇

◇◇◇◇◇◇◇◇◇◇◇◇◇◇◇◇◇◇◇◇◇◇◇◇◇◇◇◇◇◇◇◇◇◇◇◇◇◇◇◇◇◇◇◇◇◇◇◇◇◇◇◇◇◇◇◇◇ *Empower ADHD Kids!*

# Leonardo da Vinci

◇◇◇◇◇◇◇◇◇◇◇◇◇◇◇◇◇◇◇◇◇◇◇◇◇◇◇◇◇◇◇◇◇◇◇◇◇◇◇◇◇◇◇◇◇◇◇◇◇◇◇◇◇◇◇◇◇◇◇◇◇◇◇◇◇◇◇◇◇◇◇◇

## What the Experts Say

Although ADHD may make learning difficult, it can also provide a person with unique ways of seeing things that most other people cannot see. Many famous artists had difficulty learning. "Leonardo da Vinci often wrote backward; his writing shows evidence of perceptual problems." *

## Introducing the Concept

Encourage the child to seek out hidden artistic talents and explore a variety of art mediums. Use the list below and check off each one after she tries it.

| | | |
|---|---|---|
| ❑ aluminum foil sculpture | ❑ collages | ❑ feather collage |
| ❑ Indian jewelry | ❑ mosaic | ❑ stenciling |
| ❑ bean bag animals | ❑ crochet | ❑ finger painting |
| ❑ junk jewelry | ❑ murals | ❑ stitchery |
| ❑ banners | ❑ doodles | ❑ greeting cards |
| ❑ kite construction | ❑ oil paint | ❑ tie dye |
| ❑ candles | ❑ dried flower arrangement | ❑ hand print art |
| ❑ leaf print | ❑ paper sculpture | ❑ vegetable print |
| ❑ chalk drawing on sidewalk | ❑ driftwood paperweight | ❑ hat making |
| ❑ mask making | ❑ quilt | ❑ valentine cards |
| ❑ clay sculpture | ❑ egg carton project | ❑ ink blobs |
| ❑ mobiles | ❑ rock painting | ❑ water color |

## Let's Talk About It

1. Are you especially interested in creating arts and crafts?
2. Do you like making things with your hands?

## Empowering Activity

Just for fun, let the child try being like Leonardo da Vinci.

### Directions:
1. Try writing backwards. A mirror might help.
2. Try writing with the non-dominant hand.

## Empowering Messages

*Adult:* History records that many geniuses demonstrated ADHD characteristics.
*Child:* Being ADHD certainly has creative advantages.

◇◇◇◇◇◇◇◇◇◇◇◇◇◇◇◇◇◇◇◇◇◇◇◇◇◇◇◇◇◇◇◇◇◇◇◇◇◇◇◇◇◇◇◇◇◇◇◇◇◇◇◇◇◇◇◇◇◇◇◇◇◇◇◇◇◇◇◇◇◇◇◇

# Say and Do!

## What the Experts Say

Being ADHD doesn't mean that a person isn't smart. In fact, children with ADHD are often above average in intelligence. "High IQ ADD children . . . cannot only succeed in school, but may also actually enjoy it." *

## Introducing the Concept

Although many children with ADHD have above average intelligence, they often have trouble learning in conventional ways. Basically, people learn in six ways—combination of: seeing, hearing, touching, and talking. Learning is easier if the child knows which methods of learning are best suited for her.

## Let's Talk About It

1. Do you remember best by looking at something?
2. Do you remember best by hearing something?
3. Do you remember best by saying something out loud?

## Empowering Activity

Current research indicates that children with ADHD retain approximately:

| | |
|---|---|
| 10% of what they read | 50% of what they see and hear |
| 26% of what they hear | 70% of what they say |
| 30% of what they see | 90% of what they say-and-do |

On page 53 are two short stories. Use them to find out if the child learns best by hearing or by saying and doing. *(Answer key is found on page 64.)*

### Directions:

1. Read **Story One** to the child. Without looking back at the facts, have her answer the questions.
2. Next, write **Story Two** on the chalkboard or a large sheet of paper where she can look at it. This time, have her use crayons or markers to draw a picture of the parade described in the story. Using her picture, have her answer the questions.
3. Check the answers and discuss the following:
   - What percentage of questions on the first story did she answer correctly?
   - What percentage of questions on the second story did she answer correctly?
   - By percentage, how much better did she do with the say-and-do method?

## Empowering Messages

*Adult:* Experiment to see which learning methods work best for the child.

*Child:* There are many different ways to study; I will find the best method for me and use it.

# Say and Do Stories

## STORY ONE

Barbara had a dream about a parade of make-believe animals. Three yellow monkeys were walking in front of a blue-and-green striped zebra. Behind the zebra hopped four pink frogs, followed by an orange orangutan. A red lion followed directly behind the orangutan, and a giant white turtle led the parade.

### Quiz for Story One

1. What color was the animal in front of the monkeys? _____

2. How many frogs were in the parade?_____

3. What kind of animals were yellow? _____

4. What color was the animal that led the parade? _____

5. How many lions were in the parade? _____

6  How many animals were yellow? _____

7. What color was the next-to-the-last animal in the parade? _____

8. What kind of animal was striped? _____

9. What color were the animals behind the zebra? _____

10. What was the total number of animals in the parade? _____

## STORY TWO

Henry also had a dream about a parade of make-believe animals. In his parade, a purple tiger walked proudly behind two yellow ducks. Five pure white cats lead the parade and were just in front of the red-and-blue-spotted dog. Three brown-spotted snakes slithered along at the end of the parade.

### Quiz for Story Two

1. What color were the animals directly in front of the tiger? _____

2. How many turtles were in the parade? _____

3. Which animals were white? _____

4. What color were the animals that led the parade?_____

5. How many ducks were in the parade? _____

6. How many animals were brown-spotted? _____

7. What kind of animals followed the tiger? _____

8. What kind of animals had spots?_____ and _____

9. What color was the animal behind the ducks? _____

10. What was the total number of animals in the parade? _____

# KEYS TO SUCCESS #8

## Glancing Back

The lessons and activities you have just completed with your child with ADHD were designed to demonstrate that some ADHD characteristics are positive and to suggest some ways to celebrate those traits.

## Keys to Understanding ADHD

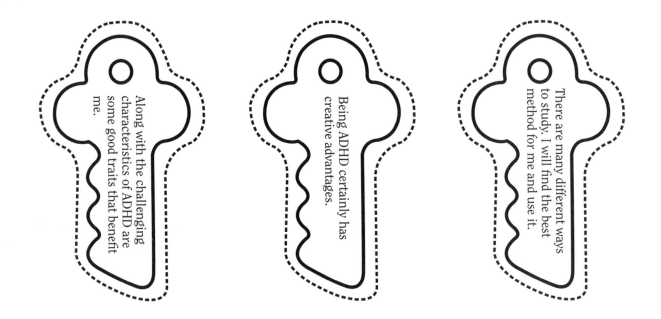

Along with the challenging characteristics of ADHD are some good traits that benefit me.

Being ADHD certainly has creative advantages.

There are many different ways to study. I will find the best method for me and use it.

## Empowering Self-Talk

Have the child copy and cut out the words below. Tell her to put them on the inside of her school notebook, use them as a bookmark, or place them inside her desk. Use the famous Shakespearean words to remind her that her most important work is being true to herself.

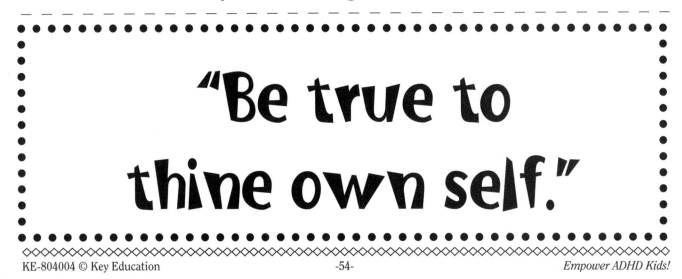

"Be true to thine own self."

# Diagnosing Self

## What the Experts Say

Although a child with ADHD can have above average intelligence, "ADD can interfere with a person's ability to demonstrate what he has learned." *

## Introducing the Concept

Intelligence accounts for at most 20 percent of the factors determining success in life. The other 80 percent consists of our ability to manage our emotions, our behaviors, and our relationships. The home and classroom are stages for practicing life skills.

## Let's Talk About It

1. How do you get along with the other students in your classroom?
2. How do you get along at home?
3. How do you get along on the playground?
4. How do you get along at play with your friends?

## Empowering Activity

It has been said that what makes human beings so intelligent is our self-awareness. Other animals do not have insight. Ask the child to stand back and observe her own life, including her patterns of learning and her relationships. In which area is she the most challenged? Ask, "If you had to describe one negative way ADHD affects your daily life, what would you say?" Discuss the specific challenge and help the child write her own recipe for living with ADHD.

1 generous helping of patience
5 cups of listening
1/2 cup of sweetness
3 armloads of kindness
lots of quiet time for reflection
20 minutes of laughter each day

## Empowering Messages

*Adult:* Even if a person is a genius, if she doesn't learn the skills needed to manage her emotions, behavior, and relationships, she will not be successful or happy.

*Child:* I can stand back and look at myself and decide what I need to do to feel good, to behave appropriately, and to have loving relationships.

# Popular People

## What the Experts Say

"Some ADD children are capable of getting their way in a not-so-abrasive manner, and this can be an asset. Maybe they'll run their own company someday!" *

## Introducing the Concept

Since children with ADHD are usually humorous and fun-loving, they are often quite social and have a lot of friends. Other children will seek their company, and very often children with ADHD are class leaders.

## Let's Talk About It

1. What makes you popular with your friends?
2. Are you a good listener? Are you empathetic?
3. Just what is it about you that your friends appreciate?

## Empowering Activity

Help the child with ADHD to recognize her strong points and learn what her friends like best about her with this ice breaker: **No "Lion," What Do You Like Best About Me?**

### Directions:

1. Enlarge the lion pattern.
2. Have the child ask her friends to autograph it and include a few words describing what they like best about the child with ADHD.

## No "Lion" What Do You Like Best About Me?

## Empowering Messages

*Adult:* Since the lives of children with ADHD are often filled with moments of hyperintensity, they need many opportunities to lighten up.

*Child:* I will seek out relaxing and fun activities and those people who appreciate me.

# Inventors

## What the Experts Say

Many children with ADHD have trouble learning in school but are regarded as curious and considered highly inventive. Learning difficulties have been overcome by some very famous inventors. "Thomas Edison couldn't learn anything in public school."*

## Introducing the Concept

At age four, Thomas Edison almost drowned while investigating a shipyard. When he grew up, his curiosity motivated him to invent more than a thousand things, including the telegraph, phonograph, incandescent lamp, and the electric railroad. Explain to the child that many famous inventors demonstrated qualities that are considered to be ADHD traits. Remind the child that thinking in a different way can lead to thoughts that no one else has ever had. ADHD might empower her to become a famous inventor.

## Let's Talk About It

1. What is an invention?
2. Do you know someone who has invented something? Who? What?
3. What do you think needs to be invented?
4. Do you sometimes think about inventing things?
5. What would you like to invent?

## Empowering Activity

Encourage creativity in the child by teaching her to brainstorm ideas. Say, "Everything had to be invented by someone. A long time ago, someone figured out that a wheel rolled. Someone else discovered that a sharp-edged stone would skin an animal and cut meat. Everything, even simple things like a cardboard box, had to be invented." Ask, "What thought process went into making a box? Do you think you can figure out how to make one?" Have a contest to see who can create a flat pattern that will fold into a three-dimensional square container.

***Directions:*** Give the child several sheets of paper, a pencil, and scissors. Encourage her to try a variety of patterns until she finds one that works.

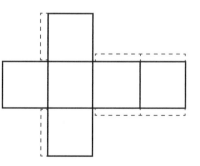

## Empowering Messages

***Adult:*** Guide the child in using her inventive nature to create new things.

***Child:*** I am inventive; I may be the next Thomas Edison just waiting to happen.

# KEYS TO SUCCESS #9

## Glancing Back ------------------------------------------------------------------------

The lessons and activities you have just completed with the child with ADHD were designed to help her understand how some ADHD characteristics are positive, and to suggest ways she can celebrate them.

## Keys to Understanding ADHD ------------------------------------------------------

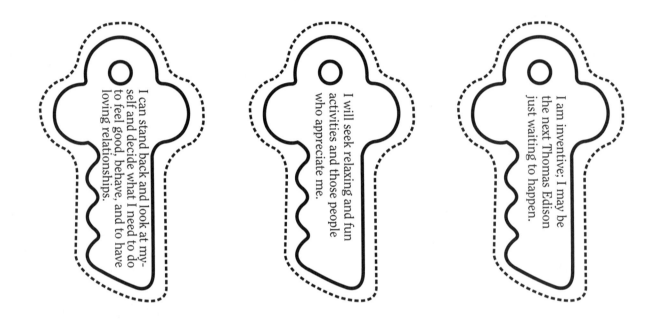

I can stand back and look at my-self and decide what I need to do to feel good, behave, and to have loving relationships.

I will seek relaxing and fun activities and those people who appreciate me.

I am inventive; I may be the next Thomas Edison just waiting to happen.

## Empowering Self-Talk -------------------------------------------------------------

Have the child copy and cut out the words below. Tell her to put them on the refrigerator door where she and her whole family will benefit from them.

I know what is best for me, and I will seek it out.

# Uniquely Me

## What the Experts Say

Everything about a child makes her uniquely herself, even the fact that she has ADHD. "Children with ADHD are typically some of the most energetic, enthusiastic, alert, creative, and perceptive students. . . ." *

## Introducing the Concept

There is no one else exactly like the child with ADHD. Even if she has a twin, she is still a unique individual. Remind the child that she cannot be perfect; no one is.

## Let's Talk About It

1. Can a person be perfect?
2. If we strive for perfection every day, how will it make us feel each time we fail?
3. Should a person always strive to do her best?
4. How is doing your best different from being perfect?
5. What are the things that make you a unique individual?

## Empowering Activity

What are the ADHD characteristics that work for the child? Has the child ever considered these or made a list of those positive characteristics? One important way to empower the child is to focus on what she can do rather than on what she can't do. The more successful she feels, the more confident she is likely to be. Provide the child with a list of her outstanding traits and accomplishments.

*Directions:* Working with the child, list all the ways she excels. Include her pleasing physical features, educational accomplishments, and the ways she is successfully dealing with her ADHD.

1. beautiful hair
2. fast runner
3. good speller
4. is learning to take turns
5. shows signs of an improving attitude about standing in line
6. likes to water ski
7. can use a computer
8. is taking kick boxing

## Empowering Messages

*Adult:* You can help build the child's self-esteem and give her the competence that she needs to overcome ADHD hurdles.

*Child:* I celebrate every aspect of myself, including the ways I am dealing with my ADHD.

# Stand Up and Take a Bow

## What the Experts Say

Most children with ADHD respond well to immediate feedback and genuine praise. "Self-help and self-healing are possible treatments . . . ." *

## Introducing the Concept

When we do a job well, we hope that others will acknowledge our efforts. This is especially true for children with ADHD. When a child with ADHD doesn't get the positive feedback that she needs, she usually will not know how to ask for it.

## Let's Talk About It

1. If you work hard and no one notices, does that make you want to quit trying?
2. If people criticize what you have done because it isn't neat enough, or isn't complete or done on time, does that make you want to stop trying?
3. When someone tells you that you did a good job, how does it make you feel?

## Empowering Activity

As parents and teachers, we are frequently not as generous with our words of appreciation as we should be. Say, "If you need acknowledgement, it is okay to ask for it. Adults do not always know what works best for you. Only you know how you feel and what you need." Teach the child how to ask for what she needs by practicing. Role-play with her and complete the following exercises.

***Directions:*** On index cards, print each of the polite ways of asking for positive feedback and/or getting needs met. Read each one to the child. Encourage her to make a stack of the ones that would work for her. Assist her in memorizing them.

1. I learn quickly through my sense of touch and I like to get pats and hugs.
2. Not knowing what is coming next worries me. Please keep me informed.
3. When I rush, I get confused and frustrated. Please allow me to go at my own pace.
4. I like to know how I am doing. Please give me immediate feedback.
5. I like to know when I am doing things the way you like me to do them. So please tell me.
6. I want to make good decisions. Help me remember to stop, think, and then act.
7. If I don't understand what you're saying, tell me again in a different way.
8. I like signals and symbols that help me know which way to go.
9. I can't always be perfect, so please praise me for my partial successes.
10. Please reward me for self-improvement.
11. Please don't yell at me. It makes me feel very sad.
12. Please give me short work periods for short-term goals.
13. I often forget my good qualities. Remind me of my good points on occasion.
14. I appreciate you as my parent or teacher; please appreciate me too.

## Empowering Messages

***Adult:*** If the child needs direction, acknowledgement, or praise and can politely ask for what she needs, make sure she is rewarded.

***Child:*** If I can clearly ask for what I need, others will be able to help me.

# Starlight Self-Talks

## What the Experts Say

If you think you can or if you think you can't, you're absolutely right. Attitude is important to success. "Many highly successful and creative people—including photo journalists, entrepreneurs, and artists—have been able to use aspects of their ADHD symptoms to great advantage." *

## Introducing the Concept

The human brain is magnificent. It listens to what we tell it about ourselves and then programs us to be that. Encourage the child to review on a regular basis the empowering messages, the keys to success, and the empowering self-talks.

## Let's Talk About It

1. List four words that describe you.
2. Which four words do you wish described you?

## Empowering Activity

Some athletes use visual imagery to practice before games. Many feel it helps them achieve their goals. Children with ADHD can benefit from positive thinking, visual imagery, and affirming self-talks, too. Have the child close her eyes and visualize herself as already having the desired traits. Also follow the exercises below for empowering self-talk.

### Directions:

1. Make a list of the four words that she says best describe her ideal self.
2. Turn the words into a poem with the guide found below.
3. Help the child memorize the poem by singing it to the tune of "Are You Sleeping, Brother John?" Example: "I am happy. I am honest. Yes, I am. Yes, I am. Also I am healthy. Also I am patient. Yes, I am. Yes, I am."
4. Encourage her to sing the tune every night, over and over, until she falls asleep. When she awakens in the middle of the night, she might be surprised to hear the happy tune still playing around and around in her head.

```
I am _____.
I am _____.
Yes, I am. Yes, I am.
Also I am _____.
Also I am _____.
Yes, I am. Yes, I am.
```

## Empowering Messages

*Adult:* In effective personal growth, visualization and positive affirmation techniques are extremely powerful in programming one's positive self.

*Child:* I can become what I choose to become.

# KEYS TO SUCCESS #10

## Glancing Back

The lessons and activities you have just completed with the child with ADHD were designed to help her understand how some ADHD characteristics are positive and give her ways to celebrate these traits.

## Keys to Understanding ADHD

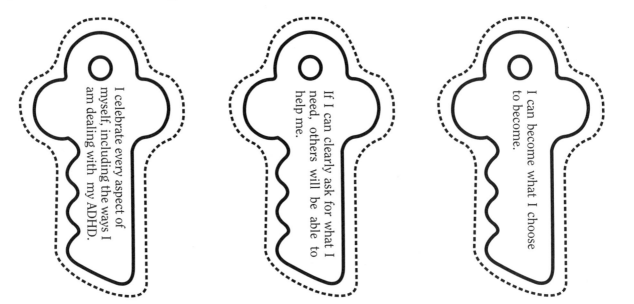

I celebrate every aspect of myself, including the ways I am dealing with my ADHD.

If I can clearly ask for what I need, others will be able to help me.

I can become what I choose to become.

## Empowering Self-Talk

Have the child copy and cut out the words below. Tell her to put them on the refrigerator door where she and her whole family will be reminded of how fantastic she is.

I am one terrific kid!

# Pre and Post Test

Have the child number the paper 1 to 25.
Read the test questions aloud. Retest after completing all the activities.

**Directions:** Mark **A** for Agree, **D** for Disagree, and **?** for Don't Know.

1. Attention deficit hyperactivity disorder (ADHD) is the most common behavioral disorder in children. _____

2. ADHD always goes away at the end of childhood. _____

3. The **A** in ADHD stands for Attention. _____

4. Some children with ADHD have great difficulty paying attention. _____

5. The first **D** in ADHD stands for deficit. _____

6. The **H** in ADHD stands for happiness. _____

7. The second **D** in ADHD stands for disease. _____

8. There is only one way to look at things—the right way. _____

9. It is especially helpful for children with ADHD to learn all about their condition. _____

10. ADHD is a secret you shouldn't tell others about. _____

11. ADHD is caused by eating too much sugar. _____

12. Children are responsible for controlling their own behavior and finding tools to help them deal with ADHD. _____

13. Parents and teachers know what distracts students. _____

14. Some children with ADHD work more slowly or more quickly than others. _____

15. Children with ADHD are not responsible for their own safety. _____

16. Children with ADHD sometimes need visual cues and special aids when learning. _____

17. Children with ADHD usually have a low level of energy. _____

18. Most children with ADHD enjoy waiting in long lines. _____

19. Children with ADHD get bored easily. _____

20. Children with ADHD are not easily angered. _____

21. Children with ADHD are often funny and have many friends. _____

22. A positive attitude is important for success. _____

23. Making a mistake is a terrible thing. _____

24. Although most children with ADHD are very smart, they sometimes have trouble learning in school. _____

25. It is empowering to take responsibility for one's self. _____

# Answer Key

**Page 19**
1. 34
2. 21
3. 35

**Page 20**
1. 10
2. 12
3. 17

**Page 28**
hippos, 11; cows, 12
cats, 14; foxes, 16

**Page 53**
Story One
1. white
2. four
3. monkeys
4. white
5. one
6. three
7. orange
8. zebra
9. pink
10. eleven

**Page 53**
Story Two
1. yellow
2. none
3. cats
4. white
5. two
6. three
7. snakes
8. dogs and snakes
9. purple
10. 12

**Page 63**
1. A
2. D
3. A
4. A
5. A
6. D
7. D
8. D
9. A
10. D
11. D
12. A
13. D

**Page 63** (con't)
14. A
15. D
16. A
17. D
18. D
19. A
20. D
21. A
22. A
23. D
24. A
25. A

# Certificate of
# Recognition
## Awarded to

_____

## an empowered ADHD kid!

**Presented by** _____

**Date** _____